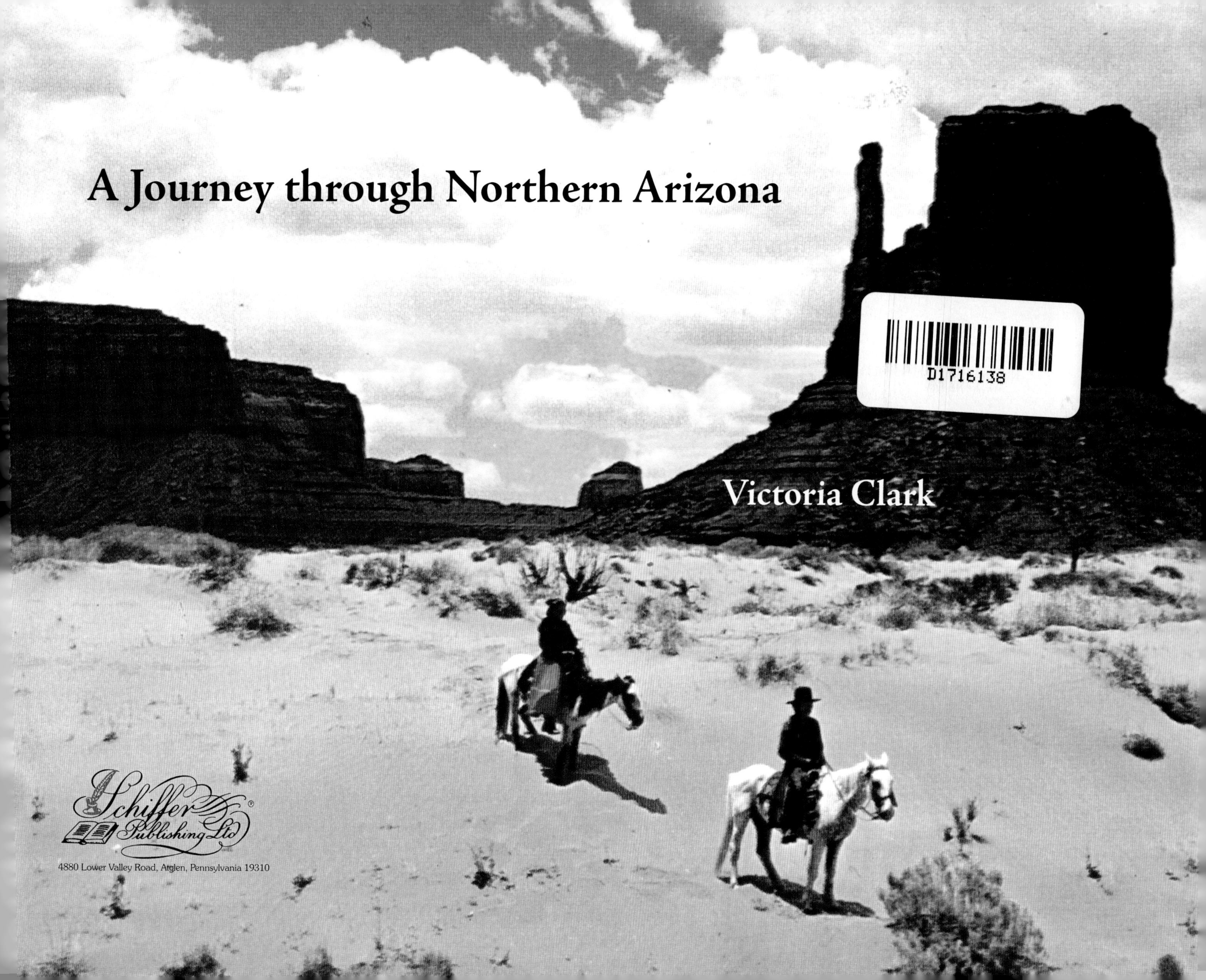
A Journey through Northern Arizona
Victoria Clark
Schiffer Publishing Ltd
4880 Lower Valley Road, Atglen, Pennsylvania 19310
D1716138

Other Schiffer Books on Related Subjects:

Scare-Izona,
978-0-7643-2844-2, $14.95

Rocky Mountain Tour,
978-0-7643-2848-0, $24.95

Bandelier National Monument: Home of the Ancestral Pueblo People
0-7643-2318-0, $12.95

BLANKET DEPARTMENT, HOTEL BEALE. KINGMAN, ARIZ.

Library of Congress Control Number: 2008927300

Designed by Stephanie Daugherty
Type set in Adobe Jenson Pro/Souvenir Lt BT/Humanist 521BT
ISBN: 978-0-7643-3010-0

Printed in China

Schiffer Books are available at special discounts for bulk purchases for sales promotions or premiums. Special editions, including personalized covers, corporate imprints, and excerpts can be created in large quantities for special needs. For more information contact the publisher:

Published by Schiffer Publishing Ltd.
4880 Lower Valley Road
Atglen, PA 19310
Phone: (610) 593-1777;Fax: (610) 593-2002
E-mail: Info@schifferbooks.com

For the largest selection of fine reference books on this and related subjects, please visit our web site at **www.schifferbooks.com**

We are always looking for people to write books on new and related subjects. If you have an idea for a book please contact us at the above address.

This book may be purchased from the publisher. Include $5.00 for shipping. Please try your bookstore first. You may write for a free catalog.

In Europe, Schiffer books are distributed by
Bushwood Books
6 Marksbury Ave.,Kew Gardens
Surrey TW9 4JF England
Phone: 44 (0) 20 8392-8585:Fax: 44 (0) 20 8392-9876
E-mail: info@bushwoodbooks.co.uk
Website: **www.bushwoodbooks.co.uk**
Free postage in the U.K., Europe; air mail at cost.

GRAND CANYON OF THE COLORADO FROM BRIGHT ANGEL POINT, NORTH RIM.

Contents

Preface

The first time I saw the Grand Canyon was in October of 1953, and I remember that I liked feeding the deer that came over to beg for our lunch better than the "giant hole" that the adults made such a fuss about. Since we lived in Tucson, playing in the fallen leaves and jumping in the patches of snow gave me a lasting impression of Northern Arizona. On that same trip, we drove though the Petrified Forest and Painted Desert, and I confess to spending most of that trip with my coloring book and crayons. In 1966, my husband and I honeymooned at the Grand Canyon, and the ever-changing beauty of the Grand Canyon has lured me back many times since then. Our family enjoyed our camping trips in Northern Arizona, and whether we were fishing in White Mountain lakes or hiking among the red rocks of Oak Creek Canyon or stopping at Cameron Trading Post, we were always aware that the people and places in Northern Arizona were unique. After wrapping up my teaching career at Pima Community College in Tucson, we chose to live in Sedona. Five years ago, I attended a meeting of the Arizona Postcard Club to learn how to store and display my ever-expanding collection of Arizona postcards. Thanks to my fellow deltiologists, both my collection and knowledge of those wonderful little "pictures" of Arizona history has continued to grow.

Introduction

Arizona is a land of glorious sunrises and sunsets. It covers an area of 113,909 miles, and was the last territory of the Continental United States to become a state on February 14, 1912. For a time, Arizona was called The Valentine State, The Baby State, and The Copper State, but now Arizona is known as The Grand Canyon State.

Northern Arizona is a study in landscape contrasts and weather extremes. A traveler can enjoy a mountainous area of tall pines and aspen, and then by traveling a short distance, view a barren desert with flat topped mesas. Northern Arizona is home to a number of Native Peoples, the Grand Canyon, the Petrified Forest the Painted Desert, the Continental Divide, Oak Creek Canyon, Hoover Dam, Route 66 towns, surreal rock spires, ancient ruins, ranches, dry farms, and trading posts.

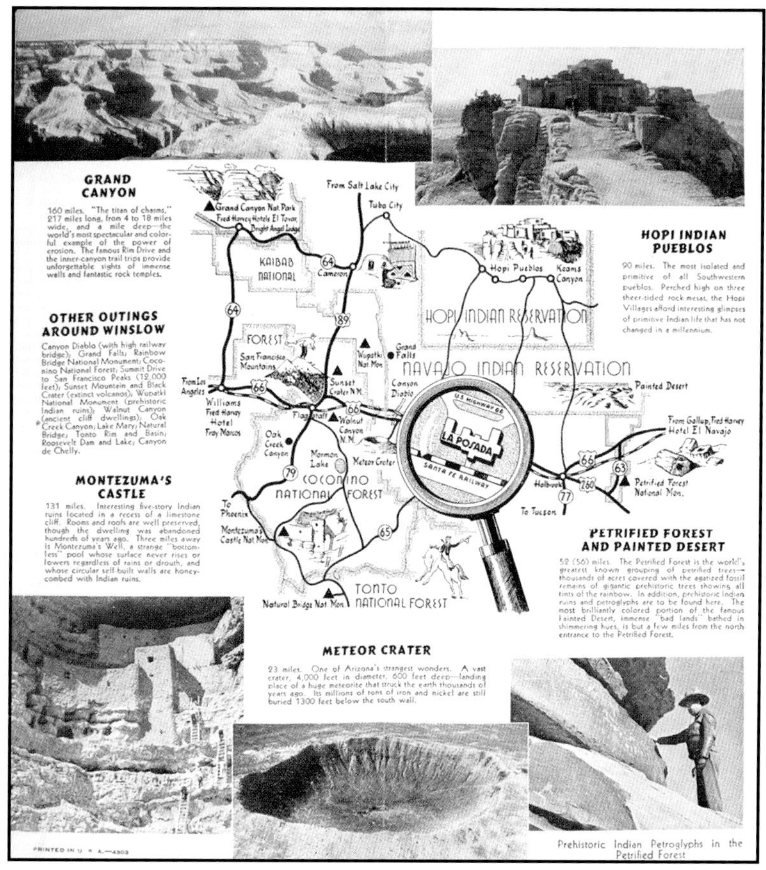

Chapter One:

Native Peoples

Hopi

The Hopi are pueblo dwellers. They have lived in Northeastern Arizona for centuries in villages high atop First, Second and Third Mesas. The Hopi pueblo of Oraibi, which is located on the Third Mesa, was established around 1100 AD. Many sources cite the Hopi pueblo of Oraibi as the oldest continuously inhabited town within the United States, and archeological studies of pottery shards found in the area date back to 1150 AD. Over a thousand residents once inhabited Oraibi. In 1540 AD, Francisco Vasquez de Coronado, who was looking for the legendary Seven Cities of Gold, led an exploration party of Spaniards that visited The Hopi. Pedro de Tovar, a member of Coronado's party, recorded the discovery of the Hopi villages. In early Spanish references, the Hopi were called Moqui, Moki, or Hopitu, which meant "the peaceful ones."

The Hopi Indian Village at Walpi, Arizona. The Walpi Hopi Pueblo is located on the First Mesa high above the Hopi farmland and desert below. C. T. Art Colortone, circa 1940s, $4-6.

Walpi Hopi Indian Pueblo, Northern Arizona. C. T. Art Colortone, circa 1940s, $4-6.

***Left:* Hopi Indians Orlin and Zellah seated on mesa above the Painted Desert. C. T. Art Colortone, circa 1940s, $4-6.**

Moqui (Hopi) Indian Home, Arizona. Berryhill, circa 1910, $8-11.

616. A Hopi Woman in Wedding Dress. Oraibi, Arizona

A Hopi Woman in Wedding Dress, Oraibi, Arizona. White buckskin moccasins and the bundle of clothing would have been a gift from her future husband. Hopi Society is organized into female-led clans. Williamson-Haffner Co., 1907, $9-12.

Kodeh, A Hopi Belle, Arizona. Her two enormous whirls of hair indicate that she is a single woman. Fred Harvey, Phostint, circa 1915, $9-12.

Hopi Indian Pueblo, Orabi, Arizona. C. T. American Art Colored, circa 1920s, $6-8.

How They Lived

Although the Hopi adopted the use of metal tools, the use of beehive ovens, the cultivation of fruit trees, and raising livestock from the Spaniards, they strongly resisted Spanish intervention and Catholicism. One theory of why the Hopi were able to keep their culture and religion was that they were more isolated geographically from Spanish rule than many of the other pueblo peoples. The Hopi believe that at one time the Creator grew so angry with mankind that He created enough water to cover the earth. Only those worthy escaped through a hole at the top of the world. The people wandered to each corner of the Americas, but then returned to the Hopi mesas. The Hopi perfected methods of dry farming, and their principle crops are corn, beans, melons, and squash. The ability to grow crops in an area that receives about ten inches of rain per year is called dry farming. Corn is at the center of many religious traditions since long ago the Hopi were given a short blue ear of corn by their spiritual ancestor Ma'saw. Corn meal is finely ground by Hopi women on metates with manos and cooked into a paper-thin bread called piki. Hunting provided rabbit, deer, and wild turkey. The Hopi believe that they are the stewards of the earth and the true messengers of land and water conservation.

Taking the Elevator, Hopi Village, Arizona. Fred Harvey, circa 1920s, $7-10.

Hopi Women Carrying Water to Tewa, Arizona.
While the Hopi live high on mesas, their gardens and orchards are on the plains below. Springs are carefully guarded. Fred Harvey, 1920, $8-10.

Hopi Mending Moccasins. Fred Harvey, Phostint, circa 1915, $7-9.

Hopi Deer Dancer.
Herz Post Cards Co., 1943, $8-11.

Hopi Reservation

In December of 1882, the United States Government set aside land for the Hopi Reservation; the Navajo Reservation surrounds the Hopi Reservation. Hopi men are the weavers and carvers while Hopi women are the basket and pottery makers. The secrets of Hopi basket weaving are passed from mother to daughter. Leaves from the yucca plant can be split as fine as thread and dyed with vegetable or aniline for basket weaving. The women from Second Mesa make coiled baskets from bear grass and yucca, while the women from Third Mesa use sumac and rabbit brush. The design of the baskets and plaques are bold, geometric patterns or figures of Kachinas also called Katsina, which represent ancestors, deities, and animals. Many Hopi ceremonies and dances are conducted according to the lunar calendar. While Kachinas are painted wooden dolls or tihu carved by the Hopi men to represent spirits, the actual ancestral Kachina spirits come in the clouds bringing life giving rain and other spiritual gifts. Hopi men, who are members of different societies according to their clan, are empowered by the Kachina spirits to visit the Hopi villages and perform various dances and ceremonies. One of the best-known ceremonies is the Hopi Snake Dance performed during the month of August. The Snake Dance is a prayer for rain and the snakes are the emissaries to the powers that bring rain. Snakes are gathered and kept in a kiva or underground spiritual chamber next to the snake alter. When the Snake Dance has been completed, the snakes are returned unharmed in keeping with Hopi philosophy to be at peace with all things. While Hopi homes may include modern conveniences, the Hopi culture has continued relatively unchanged.

Hopi Basket Dance, Arizona.
The basket dance is a nine-day ceremony conducted by the Lalakonti, a Hopi women's society. Fred Harvey, 1938, $4-6.

Hopi Pottery Maker, Grand Canyon National Park. Clay for Hopi pottery is found in the Painted Desert below the Hopi mesas. Pieces are fired and then decorated with bold geometric designs, and highly polished. Often the designs have religious significance or are imaginative interpretations of things found in nature. Fred Harvey, circa 1926, $8-10.

A Hopi Basket Weaver making baskets at Shungopovi. Published from a photograph by A. C. Vroman. Baskets are woven in a style typically found on Second Mesa. Fred Harvey, Phostint, 1903, $8-10.

Hopi Snake Altar, Walpi, Arizona.
C. T. Art Colortone, circa 1940s, $6-8.

Hopi Snake Priest entering Snake Kiva, Orabi, Arizona.
C. T. American Art-Colored, 1912, $8-10.

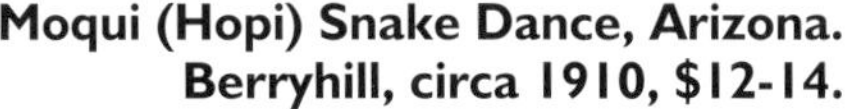

Moqui (Hopi) Snake Dance, Arizona.
Berryhill, circa 1910, $12-14.

COPYRIGHT BY C. W. WHARTON JAMES

HOPI SNAKE DANCE 35

SEE OTHER SIDE

34064

Hopi Snake Dance.
Dancers wear red-brown body paint with zigzag stripes of white and black. C. T. American Art Card, 1912, $10-12.

Navajo

The Navajo (Navaho), the largest Native American tribe, are called Dine or "the People." The seventeen million acre Navajo Reservation is located on the Colorado Plateau in Northern Arizona, but it also extends into Utah and New Mexico. Spaniards introduced horses, sheep, and cattle into the area during the sixteenth century. While horses were immediately valued for transportation, and sheep became important for both wool and meat, raising herds of cattle wasn't common practice. After the Treaty of Guadalupe Hidalgo in 1848, the United States Government formed a treaty with the Navajo leaders in 1868 to create a Navajo reservation. In return for the use of lands that bordered the reservation, the United States Government agreed to provide the Navajo with educational and medical services. Window Rock, Arizona is the capitol of the Navajo Nation. Traditionally Navajos lived in hogans, which are special multi-sided round homes constructed of cedar wood, chinked with mud, and a dirt floor. The door of the hogan was positioned to the east so that it faced the rising sun. A stove was placed in the center of the hogan, and a hole in the roof provided ventilation and exposure to the spiritual elements of the sky and air. While most Navajo today live in modern houses, a hogan is still constructed nearby for ceremonial purposes. Traditional Navajo food consists of fried bread made from dough of white flour and baking powder and fried in cooking oil, pinto beans, and mutton stew or goat, washed down with hot strong coffee. Navajo society is organized into clans.

A Navajo Sage, Arizona.
Fred Harvey, circa 1940, $6-8.

Navajo Mother and Daughters Petting Their Lambs.
C. T. Art Colortone, circa 1940s, $4-6.

"Navajo" Mother and Child. While a Fred Harvey employee forever captioned this image as a Navajo woman, she does not appear Navajo. Note that her hair is loose, her blanket isn't a Navajo pattern, and the cradleboard probably isn't Navajo. The postcard appears to be a Fred Harvey blooper. Fred Harvey, 1953, $8-12.

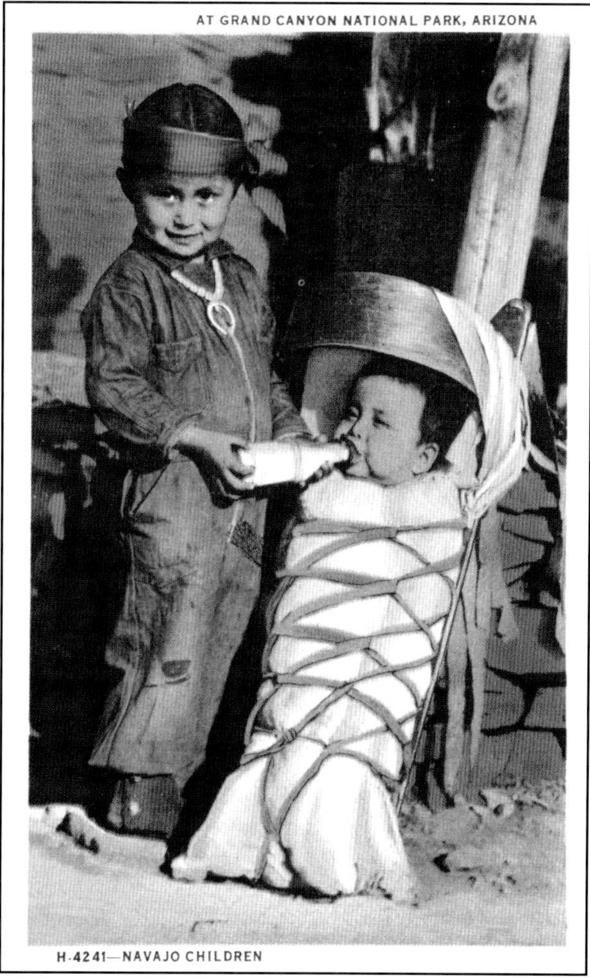

Navajo Children. Fred Harvey, circa 1940, $8-10.

Navajo Mother and Babe. Navajo children are seldom spoken to in harsh tones or punished. They are told legends to satisfy their curiosity about the world and why they should or should not do certain things. C. T. Art Photocolor, 1944, $7-9.

The Silversmith's Daughter.
The adorable little girl is wearing traditional Navajo jewelry made from coin silver and turquoise by her father. C. T. Art Colortone, circa 1940s, $7-9.

Navajo Chicken Pull. Since chickens were often not available, filled burlap bags with one corner exposed were used to demonstrate a rider's horsemanship skills. Detroit Publishing Co., Phostint, 1907, $10-12.

A Navajo Poker Game, Arizona.
The Bureau of Indian Affairs once had laws against gambling on reservations. Trading posts could not sell playing cards or dice, but these Navajo men are enjoying the game. Williamson-Haffner Co., circa 1907, $10-12.

Loom Weaving

Navajos are well known for their loom weaving of fine, colorful blankets, and rugs. Many visitors are surprised at the prices of these beautiful works, until they understand the hours of labor it takes to sheer, clean, card, and spin the wool into yarn, even before the loom is prepared with the proper warp. Countless hours are spent in weaving the intricate patterns. Specific patterns and colors of rugs differ according to the region where they were woven and the clan of the weaver. Navajos are also well known artists for their silver jewelry set with turquoise and other semi-precious stones. Jewelry and other items were created from melting American silver coins until the United States Government passed laws against destroying or defacing coins. While 3,600 Navajos served in the Armed Forces during World War II and the services of the Navajo Code Talkers were invaluable, it wouldn't be until 1948 that Arizona's Native Peoples would have the right to vote.

**Navajo Rug Weaver.
C. T. Art Colortone, circa 1940s, $6-8.**

**Navajo Blanket Weavers.
While one woman weaves, another is spinning sheep wool into yarn. A young girl is helping to clean and card the wool. Detroit Publishing Co., Phostint, circa 1910, $8-10.**

D-51 THE STORY OF THE NAVAJO RUG

© C. T. CO. 4A-H1126

The Story of the Navajo Rug.
Sheep graze nearby while a mother weaves and her daughters work to prepare the yarn. C. T. Art Colortone, circa 1940s, $6-8.

Navajo Indian Silversmith, Da Pah, Plying His Trade.
Da Pah is wearing a traditional silver squash blossom necklace that represents fertility, and the crescent at the bottom of the necklace is said to have come from the naja as an amulet to ward off the evil eye. C. T. American Art Colored, 1938, $5-7.

Navajo Drilling Turquoise.
C. T. Art Colored, circa 1940s, $4-6.

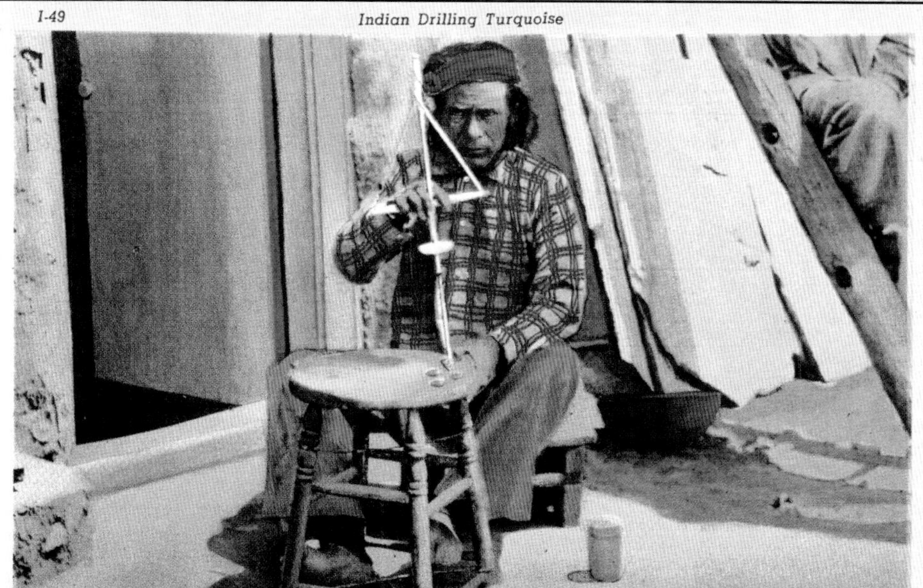

Navajo Hogan. C. T. Art Colortone. Circa 1940s, $6-8.

Navajo Family in front of Hogan on Reservation. C. T. Art Colortone, 1940, $6-8.

Navajo Sand Painters. Many colors of fine sand are used to create a Navajo sand painting for ceremonial purposes such as a healing. Natural Color Card. A Western Ways photograph by Ray Manley, 1952, $3-6.

Canyon de Chelley

Canyon de Chelley is a twenty-seven mile long canyon formed of petrified sand dunes located near Chinle in the heart of Navajo land. It was in Canyon de Chelley that the Navajos made their last stand against the United States Army before their march to Fort Sumner. On the floor of Canyon de Chelley, Navajos farm corn, pumpkins, squash, beans, peaches, and apples. It is a sacred place and religious ceremonies such as the Blessingway are held there. Around four hundred separate ruins exist in and around Canyon de Chelley, and the White House Ruin is the largest. The White House Ruin, so named for its white plastered walls, was built by the Anasazi and is believed to have had eighty rooms and forty kivas. Spider Rock is an eight hundred foot sandstone monolith in Canyon de Chelley. It is the sacred place where Spider Woman lives. Navajos believe that Spider Woman taught Navajo women how to weave, while Spider Man taught them how to build a loom. Navajo children are taught that Spider Woman herself might appear and eat children who are naughty.

The White House Ruins in Canyon de Chelley. C. T. American Art, 1946, $4-6.

Central Navajo Indian Agency Window Rock. Looking through the "TseGah ho Tzun" or Hole in the Rock. The hole, now called Window Rock, is worn away Dakota sandstone. The surrounding area is also known as Window Rock and government offices can be seen below. Window Rock is the "nee Aineeng" or center of Navajoland. C. T. Art Colortone, circa 1940s, $4-6.

Navaho Horsemen in Canyon de Chelley, Arizona. Fred Harvey, circa 1920s, $5-7.

A Navajo Sheep Herder Canyon de Chelley. C. T. Art Colortone, circa 1940s, $4-6.

Canyon de Chelley, *New Mexico (Territory). This card was issued before Arizona's statehood. Fred Harvey, Phostint, circa 1905, $5-7.

The Hubble Trading Post

During the 1870s, John Lorenzo Hubble Sr. and his family had established several trading posts on the Navajo reservation. The trading post at Ganado was the Hubble family home and farm of 160 acres, which Hubble had claimed under the Homestead Act. In 1886, during an epidemic of smallpox, Hubble turned his home into an infirmary. Hubble envisioned a mission at Ganado with a school and a hospital, and in 1901, Hubble encouraged the Presbyterian Church to establish a mission. The Hubble Trading Post is now the oldest continuously operated trading post on the Navajo Reservation, and it is a National Historic site and museum operated by the National Park Service. The museum displays a number of ancient Navajo rugs and other Hopi and Navajo crafts, as well as other historic pioneer items from the region. Many religious groups built schools and missions for native peoples; however, the Ganado Presbyterian Mission, which included a church, school, hospital, and a school of nursing, became the largest and most well-known reservation mission in the United States.

Sage Memorial Hospital, Ganado Mission, Ganado, Arizona. Artvue Post Card Co., circa 1937, $5-7.

Overview of the Ganado Trading Post, Farm, Mission, School, and Hospital. RPPC, 1947, $7-9.

Clarence G. Salsbury High School Building, Ganado Mission, Ganado, Arizona. Artvue Post Card Co., circa 1937, $5-7.

Entrance to Ganado Presbyterian Church, Ganado, Arizona.
Artvue Post Card Co., circa 1937, $5-7.

Ganado Presbyterian Church, Ganado Mission, Ganado, Arizona.
Artvue Post Card Co., circa 1937, $5-7.

The Dining Hall, Ganado Mission, Ganado, Arizona.
Artvue Post Card Co., circa 1937, $5-7.

Other Tribes

The White Mountain Apache are closely related to other Western Apache Nations such as the Chiricahua, Mescalero, Jicarrilla, and Kiowa-Apache, even though there are differences in language and history. Early Apache roamed Arizona in family groups, farming, hunting and gathering native foods. Thin strips of venison, elk, bear, buffalo, and beef were dried for jerky. The Apache both traded and raided. When the United States Army began settling the White Mountain area in Northeastern Arizona, orders were given to capture or kill the Apache. In 1891, Apache leaders agreed to the creation of a military fort along the confluence of the East and North Forks of the White River, and the establishment of the Fort Apache Indian Reservation. The fort known as Fort Apache would remain in use until 1922, after which time it became home to the Bureau of Indian Affairs for the Apache and the Theodore Roosevelt Indian Boarding School. While originally Fort Apache included the San Carlos Reservation, Congress voted to separate the two in 1897.

Apache Maiden, Fort Apache Indian Reservation. Maiden is wearing a handmade buckskin cape and camp dress worn for the traditional "coming out ceremony" for young Apache girls. Norm's Publishing House, circa 1953, $4-6.

Apache Indians as seen in Arizona. RPPC, 1950, $10-12.

White Mountain Apache Girl, Arizona. Williamson-Haffner Co., circa 1920, $8-10.

White Mountain Apache Hoops and Javelin Game, Arizona. Williamson-Haffner, circa 1907, $10-15.

An Apache Chief in Camp.
Detroit Publishing Co., Phostint, circa 1913, $7-9.

Apache Indian and Child, Arizona. Harry Herz.
C. T. American Art Colored, circa 1943, $7-9.

The Havasupai

The Havasupai (later shortened to Supai), which means "people of the blue green water," were living in the area south of the western end of the Grand Canyon as early as 1300 AD. Their reservation was established in 1880 on land along Havasu Creek, which has three high waterfalls, turquoise colored pools, and dense vegetation. The waterfalls have always attracted visitors who must hike into the remote "Canyon of the Sky Blue Water." During the summer months, the Supai constructed summer homes of cedar boughs, bark, and juniper, and they were employed to work on the early roads and trails in the Grand Canyon. Traditional Supai women wear their hair cut straight across the forehead and the back of their hair is cut into a shoulder length bob.

On the Havasupai Indian Reservation, Arizona.
Fred Harvey, Phostint, 1930, $7-9.

S. 90(B) Navajo Falls, 60 ft. high, (Copyrighted) Cataract Canon,

Navajo Falls, sixty feet high in Cataract Canyon.
T. Stith Baldwin, 1908, $10-12.

H-2243 SUPAI SQUAW WEAVING BASKET, CATARACT CANYON, ARIZONA

Supai Weaving Coiled Willow Basket, Cataract Canyon, Arizona. Fred Harvey, Phostint, circa 1915, $12-15.

The Hualapai

Peach Springs located near the west end of the Grand Canyon is the tribal headquarters of the Hualapai (also spelled Walapai), which means "people of the tall pine." Traditional Hualapai speak Yuman, and historically the Haulapai lived in conical houses built from cedar boughs called wikieups. Peach Springs was once a Santa Fe Railroad center and many of the old Fred Harvey buildings remain. Route 66 crosses through Peach Springs, which has been a commercial center for the Hualapai, as well as a government center.

O. C. Osterman Auto Court, Peach Springs, Arizona, on US Route 66. C. T. Photo Platin, circa 1935, $8-10.

A Walapai Indian Woman. Rapheal Tuck & Sons, "England Oilette Indian Women Series," circa 1910, $15-20.

Hualapai Pow-Wow, Peach Springs, Arizona. Albertype Co., circa 1930, $25-30.

**Walapai Indian Woman and Child.
Raphael Tuck & Sons, "England Oilette Native Arizonans Series," circa 1910, $15-20.**

Ruins

From the most primitive remnants of pit dwellings to the most sophisticated multistory villages, ruins of those who came before us have always been an attraction for visitors and archaeologists. Disturbing ruins and the artifacts found there is to unbalance the universe, according to Ramon Riley, the White Mountain Apache Cultural Resources Director. While scientists see the ruins and artifacts as scientific objects to yield clues to past civilizations, Native Americans see these places and objects as connections to the spiritual having been consecrated by many prayers.

Montezuma Well, Arizona. R. L Balke Indian Trading Co., circa 1925, $5-7

Montezuma's Castle

Montezuma's Castle is a five-story, cliff dwelling one hundred feet above Beaver Creek in the Verde Valley. The cliff overhang has protected the ruin for centuries. Montezuma's Castle was built by the Sinagua Indians sometime around 1150 AD using tools of sharpened stone, bone, and wood. Sycamore ceiling beams support the foot-thick rock walls. The name Montezuma's Castle is a misnomer, since Montezuma, the Aztec Ruler, never visited the ruin. The Sinaguas, whose name in Spanish means "without water," were excellent farmers and highly skilled at developing irrigation systems. In addition to Beaver Creek below Montezuma's Castle, another source of water was Montezuma's Well, a natural red wall limestone, fifty-five foot deep sinkhole, located eleven miles north. While the exact source of the water flowing into Montezuma's Well is somewhat of a mystery, every twenty-four hours 1.4 to 1.5 million gallons of water rush into the well. It is believed that about 150 people lived there in 1300 AD, but by the time the Spanish explorer Antonio de Espejo and his men were led to the ruin by a group of Pueblo Indians in 1583, the area was deserted.

Montezuma Ancient Cliff Dwellers. E. C. Kropp Co., circa 1938, $4-6.

Montezuma's Castle, Arizona. Harry Herz. C. T. American Art Colored, circa 1930, $6-8.

Walnut Canyon

Walnut Canyon National Monument is located about seven miles from Flagstaff. Over time, the tiny Walnut Creek carved a six hundred foot deep canyon into the limestone rock walls. The erosion created a series of small caves that were used by the Sinagua as dwellings. Shards of pottery and other remains found in Walnut Canyon indicate that the Sinagua lived there as early as 1100 AD. The Sinauga dressed in skins, crafted simple black and white pottery, farmed, gathered, hunted, and extracted medicines from plants, cacti, and pines. The overhang of cliffs offered protection from the elements. The walls of the cliff dwellings were constructed of mud, stone, and rough timber. Over three hundred ruins have been discovered in Walnut Canyon, but only a few are accessible to the public. A unique discovery about the ruins in Walnut Canyon is that archeologists believe that each ruin had six to eight rooms and was meant to house separate families instead of communal usage. Walnut Canyon became a National Monument in 1915.

Cliff Dwelling with T Doorway, Island Trail, Walnut Canyon National Monument, Arizona. RPPC, circa 1950, $10-12.

Cliff Dwelling Ruins, Walnut Canyon National Monument, Arizona. RPPC, circa 1950, $10-12.

Cliff dwellings,
Walnut Canyon Near Flagstaff, Arizona.
C. T. American Art Card, circa 1930s, $4-6.

Cliff dwellings,
Walnut Canyon near Flagstaff, Arizona.
C. T. American Art, circa 1930s, $4-6.

Ancient Cliff Dwellings,
Walnut Canyon, Northern Arizona.
C. T. American Art Colored. Herz,
circa 1930s, $4-6.

Southern Unit of Wupat ki Ruin,
Wupatki National Monument, Arizona.
C. T. Art Colortone, circa 1950, $7-9.

The Wupatki National Monument

The Wupatki National Monument is located about thirty-five miles north of Flagstaff and consists of three ruins: Nalakihu, Teuwalanki, and Wupatki. Wupatki means "tall house" in Hopi, and it is the largest above-ground ruin built by the ancient Anasazi people who lived there during the 1100s AD. The walls were built of natural red MoenKopi sandstone. The pueblo was known to have one hundred rooms and a ball court. The Wupatki continues to puzzle archeologists as they speculate about what could have drawn the Anasazi to this harsh remote place where there would have been hot blistering days in the summer and freezing cold in the winter and little available water. The ruin is visited by members of the Hopi, Zuni, and Navajo tribes who consider the people who once lived at Wupatki their spiritual ancestors.

Southern Unit of Wupatki Ruin,
Wupatki National Monument, Arizona.
C. T. Art Colortone, circa 1950, $7-9.

Chapter Two:

Scenic Wonderland

The Painted Desert near Adamana, Arizona.

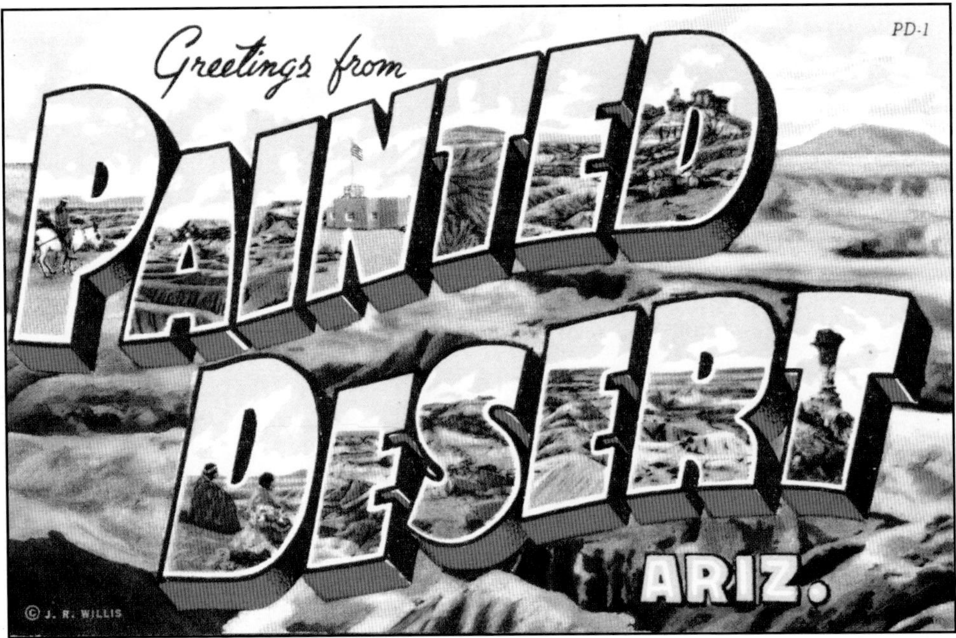

Greetings from Painted Desert, Arizona.
C. T. Art Colortone, circa 1940s, $5-7.

Painted Desert

The Painted Desert is located across Northern Arizona extending from the Grand Canyon National Park on the western end, and bordered by the Petrified Forest National Park on the eastern end. Many ancient cultures have lived in the arid area. The Painted Desert covers approximately 93,533 acres, and vegetation is extremely sparse. Colored sand from The Painted Desert has been used for centuries by the Native Peoples for sand paintings.

The Painted Desert.
C. T. Art Colortone, circa 1940s, $4-6.

Near the Black Forest Painted Desert, Arizona. C. T. American Art Colored. Harry Herz, circa 1930, $4-6.

The Painted Desert, Arizona. Albertype Co., circa 1925, $8-10.

The Painted Desert near Adamana, Arizona. Albertype Co., published for the Rainbow Lodge, circa 1925, $8-10.

The Landscape

The Spaniards were the first to call the area "El Desierto Pintura" because of the many brightly colored layers of stratified minerals that appeared like layers of paint on a canvas. The landscape consists of dunes, mesas, and sandstone columns in surrealistic shapes that have been formed by centuries of erosion caused by wind and water. At sunrise and sunset, the amount of light intensifies the colors of blue, violet, orange-red, gold, and grey. Red is the predominant color from hematite, and the yellows are from limonite. Evidence of fossil tracks, fossils, and bones from extinct animals, reptiles, and amphibians are found in the area.

The Painted Desert, Arizona.
The multi colored sands change colors throughout the day.
C. T. Art Colortone, circa 1940s, $4-6.

The Painted Desert, Arizona.
One can travel from Gallup, New Mexico and Holbrook, Arizona where wonderful views of the Painted Desert can be seen from the highway.
C. T. Art Colortone, circa 1940s, $4-6.

The Painted Desert, Arizona.
C. T. Art Colortone, circa 1940s, $4-6.

The Painted Desert, Arizona — a desert of multicolored sands, rocks, and petrified wood interspersed with fantastic erosions.
C. T. Art Colortone, circa 1940s, $4-6.

Painted Desert Inn, Arizona. Fred Harvey, circa 1953, $6-8.

The Painted Desert Inn

The Painted Desert Inn was built by Herbert Lore in 1924 and given the name The Stone Tree House. The Inn was built on a high point that provided a vantage view for visitors to overlook the Painted Desert. Lore used native materials of rock and chunks of petrified wood. While tiny, the Painted Desert Inn had a lunchroom, a bar, six tiny rooms, and a gift shop. Lore sold the property and in 1945, the Inn was transferred to the Fred Harvey Company. The Painted Desert Inn was a departure from Harvey's other hotels that were connected to the Santa Fe Railroad; however, automobile traffic was increasing along the nearby Route 66 corridor, while train travel was declining. Mary Jane Coulter, an architect for the Fred Harvey Company, supervised the renovation of the Inn and Hopi artist Fred Kabotie was commissioned to paint murals on the walls. The Inn survived not only a fire in 1953, but also several times, it narrowly escaped demolition. However, in 1976, the National Park Service reopened the former inn as a museum and travel information center. The site was designated a National Historic Landmark in October of 2004.

Painted Desert Inn, on the Edge of the Painted Desert near Holbrook, Arizona. RPPC, S.W. Postcard Co., circa 1953, $12-14.

Painted Desert Inn, Arizona.
C. T. Art Colortone, circa 1926, $6-8.

Trading Post on rim of Painted Desert Park, Arizona.
C. T. Art Colored, circa 1940s, $8-10.

Lobby of Painted Desert Inn, Arizona.
C. T. American Art Colored, circa 1930, $10-12.

Petrified Forest

The Petrified Forest is located twenty-five miles east of Holbrook. While some visitors are disappointed not to see upright stone trees, or a lush forest, the fallen trees that petrified or turned to stone from being underwater millions of years ago offer a variety of rainbow colors. The surrounding layers of earth hardened into sandstone and shale of the Chinle Formation. Early visitors would stop at the small town of Adamana to write their names in a guest book and drive through the Petrified Forest by picking the most traveled tire tracks. The Petrified Forest has a number of petroglyphs and ruins from the Native peoples who used the petrified wood to build simple shelters. Because souvenir hunters threatened the area, the Petrified Forest was made a National Monument in 1906, and a National Park in 1962.

Greetings from Petrified Forest, Arizona. C. T. Art Colortone, circa 1940s, $6-9.

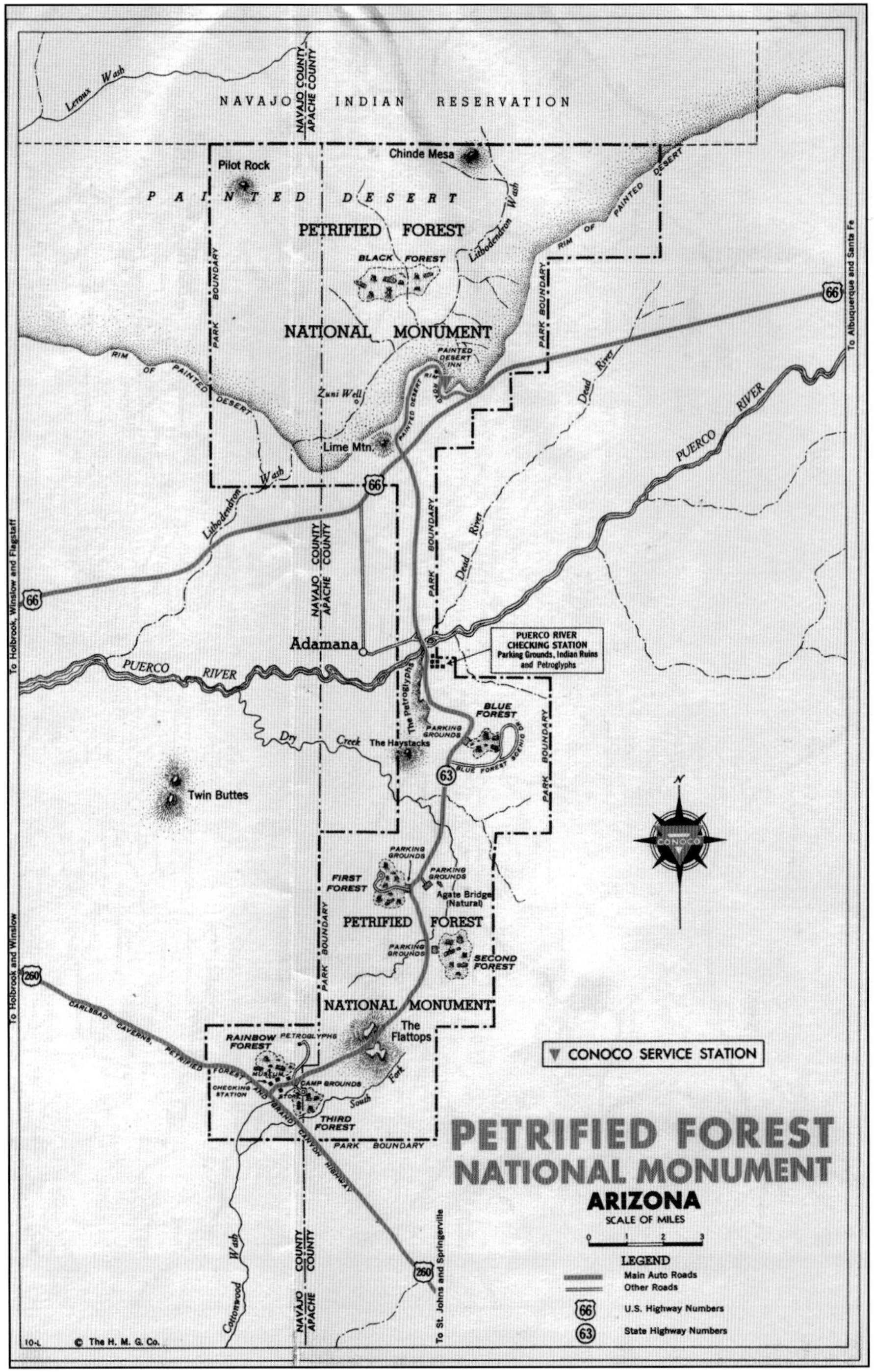

NAVAJO INDIAN RESERVATION
NAVAJO COUNTY
APACHE COUNTY
Pilot Rock
Chinde Mesa
PAINTED DESERT
PETRIFIED FOREST
BLACK FOREST
NATIONAL MONUMENT
PAINTED DESERT INN
Zuni Well
Lime Mtn.
RIM OF PAINTED DESERT
PARK BOUNDARY
Adamana
PUERCO RIVER
PUERCO RIVER CHECKING STATION
Parking Grounds, Indian Ruins and Petroglyphs
The Petroglyphs
Dry Creek
The Haystacks
BLUE FOREST
PARKING GROUNDS
Twin Buttes
FIRST FOREST
Agate Bridge (Natural)
PETRIFIED FOREST
SECOND FOREST
NATIONAL MONUMENT
The Flattops
RAINBOW FOREST
PETROGLYPHS
CHECKING STATION
CAMP GROUNDS
THIRD FOREST
CARLSBAD CAVERNS, PETRIFIED FOREST AND GRAND CANYON HIGHWAY
Cottonwood Wash
To Holbrook, Winslow and Flagstaff
To Holbrook and Winslow
To Albuquerque and Santa Fe
To St. Johns and Springerville
CONOCO SERVICE STATION

PETRIFIED FOREST
NATIONAL MONUMENT
ARIZONA
SCALE OF MILES
LEGEND
Main Auto Roads
Other Roads
U.S. Highway Numbers
State Highway Numbers

© The H. M. G. Co.

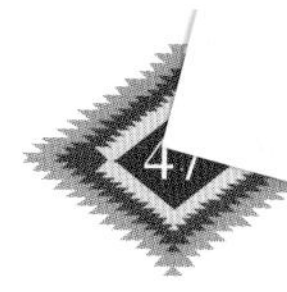

Natural Bridge in the Petrified Forest, Adamana, Arizona. Albertype Co., circa 1920, $7-9.

Petrified Forest, Arizona. Albertype Co., 1917, $20-22.

Petrified Bridge, Petrified Forest, Arizona. Visitors sitting on the petrified log bridge give perspective to the size of the giant log. B Co., circa 1918, $10-12.

The Bad Lands, Petrified Forest, Arizona.
Fred Harvey Co., Phostint, circa 1930s, $4-6

Eagle Rock Petrified Forest, Arizona.
This hoodoo formed by wind, rain, and giant dust clouds is known as Eagle's Nest. Hand-colored, Albertype Co., circa 1910, $10-12.

The Snow Lady, Petrified Forest near Holbrook, Arizona.
Hand-colored, Albertype Co., circa 1920, $10-12.

Petroglyphs, Prehistoric Indian Picture Writing, Petrified Forest National Monument, Arizona. RPPC, Frasher's Fotos, circa 1953, $7-9.

Campbell's Hotel Adamana, Arizona.
Sign painted on roof of hotel: "Petrified Forest, 6 Miles, Painted Desert, 9 Miles." Albertype Co., circa 1920, $10-12.

Agate House Prehistoric Indian Ruins, Petrified Forest, Arizona. RPPC, circa 1950, $12-15.

Petrified Wood

The colors commonly found in the petrified wood are red from hematite, yellow from limonite, and white from gypsum. Although it is forbidden to take petrified wood, vandals have literally carried tons of petrified wood home with them. When the chunks of agate and carnelian have been cut and polished, they become beautiful semi-precious stones used for jewelry, bookends, and doorstops. In the area called the Crystal Forest, the logs once held crevices of clear quartz and purple amethyst crystals, but these have been removed by souvenir hunters. Looters and vandals have continued to rob the park of its artifacts and petrified wood. A legend exists that warns removing petrified wood is bad luck, so every year some of the rocks that have been taken are mailed or brought back with letters of apology.

Petrified Wood and Erosions, Petrified Forest, Arizona. C. T. Art Colortone, circa 1940s, $4-6.

The Arm Chair, Petrified Forest, Arizona near the Natural Bridge. Log is resting on a stone formation. C. T. Art Colortone, circa 1940s, $5-7.

Giant Logs in Rainbow Forest, Petrified Forest.
Some trees are over two hundred feet in length and display all the colors of the rainbow. C. T. Art Colortone, circa 1940s, $4-6.

The Twin Sisters in Second Forest, Petrified Forest, Arizona.
C. T. Art Colortone, circa 1940s, $4-6.

Logs of Stone, Petrified Forest, Arizona.
C. T. Art Colortone, circa 1940s, $4-6.

Nez by Big Log, Petrified Forest, Arizona. Compare the size of the log with Nez, who is 6'2 inches tall. C. T. Art Colortone, circa 1940s, $4-6.

Agatized Logs, Petrified Forest, Arizona. C. T. Art Colored, circa 1940s, $4-6

Meteor Crater, the Grave of Arizona's Giant Meteor; width is 4,150 feet, the depth, 570 feet. RPPC, circa 1953, $7-9.

Meteor Crater

Meteor Crater is the second largest crater on earth. It's located thirty-five miles east of Flagstaff and twenty miles west of Winslow. It's estimated that the meteorite impacted Earth there approximately 49,000 years ago. Native Peoples in the area knew of the site centuries ago, and created legends about its existence. The area was discovered by white men as early as 1871 and around 1886, sheepherders found meteorites from the crater near Canyon Diablo. At that time, theories were formulated that the crater had been created by volcanic activity. In 1902, Daniel Moreau Barringer, a mining engineer from Philadelphia, took possession of the crater and conducted scientific studies on the crater for the next twenty-five years. During that time, Barringer drilled and searched for the large body of ore that he believed was a meteorite beneath the crater, but again and again, he was disappointed. By 1929, Barringer had correctly adjusted his thinking to believe that the meteorite must be higher up about one hundred feet somewhere along the south rim. After his last attempt at drilling jammed the bit, his funds were depleted and his experiments ceased. While Barringer never realized his goal to find the meteorite, he was recognized as the first person to prove that large chunks of matter were capable of entering the Earth's orbit and impacting Earth. It's ironic that, years later, the mass of ore was discovered using modern equipment right where Barringer had last drilled. Meteor Crater is a private attraction still owned by descendents of the Barringer family. Meteor Crater attracts those with an interest in astronomy, and those who believe in UFOs. Because the surface of Meteor Crater resembles the lunar landscape, some of the Apollo astronauts trained there. Meteor Crater was one of the most visited tourist attractions on Route 66 during the 1940s and 1950s.

Aerial View of Meteor Crater.
The road to the Observation Point of the Crater's Rim is shown.
Frasher's Fotos, circa 1951, $8-10.

H-3971 METEORITE CRATER NEAR WINSLOW, ARIZONA

Meteorite Crater near Winslow, Arizona.
The slopes are covered with boulders and crushed rock. Fred Harvey, circa 1940s, $4-6.

Monument Valley

Monument Valley is located along the Arizona/Utah border, and is now a Navajo Tribal park. John Ford helped to popularize Monument Valley in 1939, when his Western film "Stagecoach" starring John Wayne was released. The large natural sandstone rock formations appear as giant sculptures. Distance and space seem endless in Monument Valley. The Mittens, the Three Sisters, the Thumb, and the Totem Pole are among the most visited and photographed formations. To the north of Monument Valley is Rainbow Bridge, a natural stone bridge formed over time by the forces of wind and water. While for many years Rainbow Bridge was too remote to be seen by many visitors, the creation of Lake Powell allows access to the bridge by boat.

Rainbow Natural Bridge.
RPPC, Frasher's Fotos, circa 1950, $5-7.

Rainbow Natural Bridge.
The natural stone bridge is 308 feet high and has a span of 274 feet.
Herz Post Cards, circa 1940s, $4-6.

Monument Valley, Arizona. Petley, circa 1956, $3-5.

The Mittens in Monument Valley.
Buttes and pinnacles of red sandstone rising 1,100 feet above the shifting desert sand.
C. T. Art Colored, circa 1940s, $4-6.

Grand Canyon

The Grand Canyon was carved over millennia by erosion, and it is one of the most colorful, awe-inspiring landscapes on earth. The Grand Canyon is approximately 270 million years old, one mile deep, eighteen miles wide and 277 miles long. The area was known and occupied by Native Peoples for thousands of years; however, the Spanish explorer Garcia Lopez de Cardenas with a small party of men took credit for its "discovery" somewhere along the South Rim in 1540. When the area became part of the New Mexico Territory in 1850, it seemed largely unimportant except to traders and trappers. In 1869, John Wesley Powell, a one-armed Civil War veteran, gathered a small company of men to explore and make a geological survey of the Colorado River and the surrounding canyons. Artist Thomas Moran's painting of the "Chasm of the Colorado" and his illustrations of Powell's report focused new attention on the mighty Colorado River and the Grand Canyon. The Grand Canyon was declared a forest preserve by proclamation of President Benjamin Harrison in 1893, and President Teddy Roosevelt established the Grand Canyon as a game preserve and then as a national monument. During the presidency of Woodrow Wilson, the Grand Canyon became the Grand Canyon National Park in 1919.

Down Granite Gorge from Bright Angel Trail, Grand Canyon, Arizona. Detroit Photographic Co., 1902, $7-9.

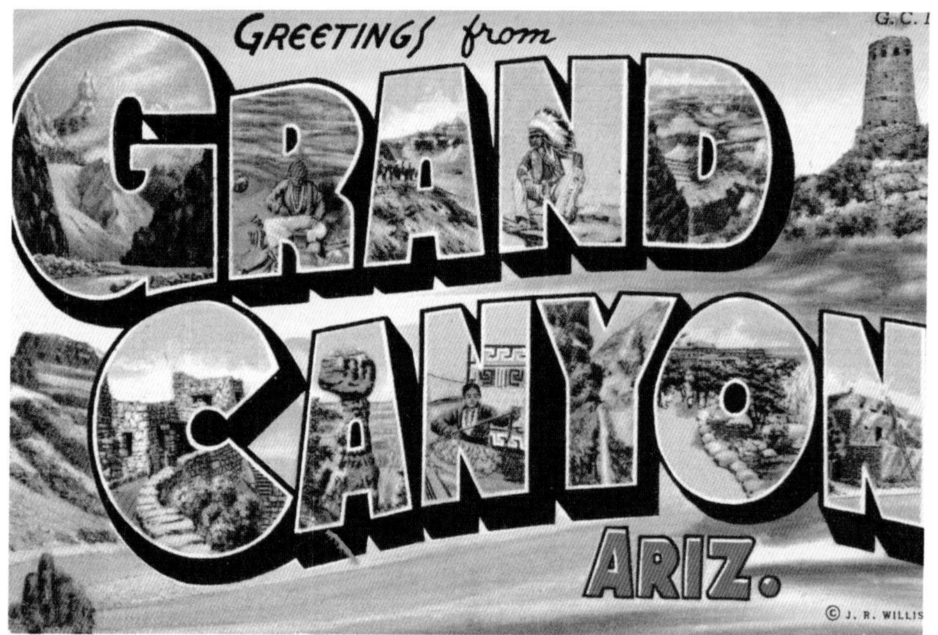

Greetings from Grand Canyon, Arizona. C. T. Art Colortone, circa 1940s, $5-7.

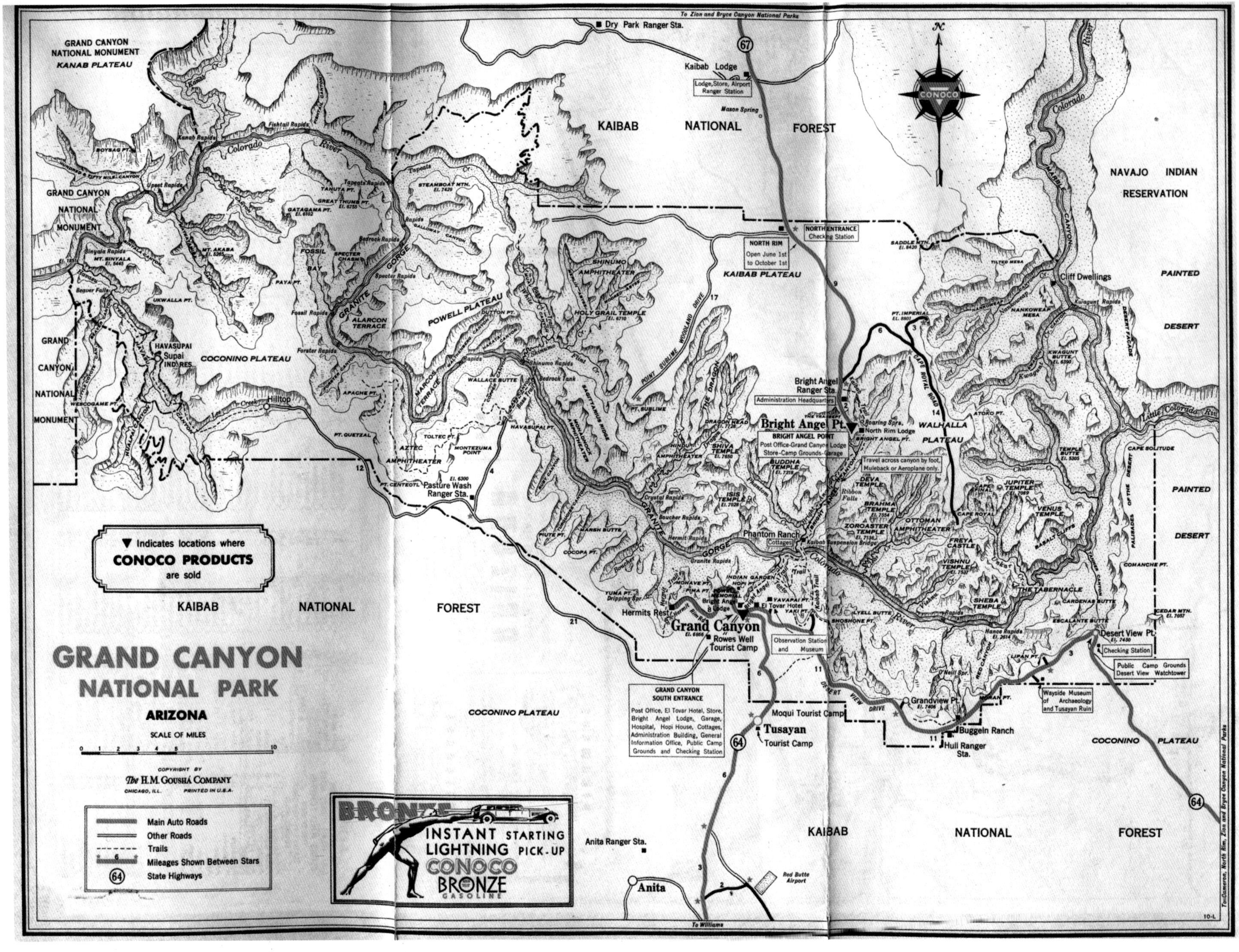

GRAND CANYON NATIONAL PARK

ARIZONA

SCALE OF MILES

0 1 2 3 4 5 10

COPYRIGHT BY
The H. M. GOUSHÁ COMPANY
CHICAGO, ILL. PRINTED IN U.S.A.

▼ Indicates locations where
CONOCO PRODUCTS
are sold

Main Auto Roads
Other Roads
Trails
Mileages Shown Between Stars
State Highways

To Zion and Bryce Canyon National Parks

Dry Park Ranger Sta.

Kaibab Lodge

Lodge, Store, Airport
Ranger Station

Mason Spring

KAIBAB NATIONAL FOREST

CONOCO

NAVAJO INDIAN RESERVATION

GRAND CANYON NATIONAL MONUMENT

KANAB PLATEAU

NORTH ENTRANCE
Checking Station

NORTH RIM
Open June 1st
to October 1st

KAIBAB PLATEAU

Cliff Dwellings

PAINTED DESERT

POWELL PLATEAU

SHINUMO AMPHITHEATER

HOLY GRAIL TEMPLE

COCONINO PLATEAU

HAVASUPAI
Supai
IND. RES.

Hilltop

Bright Angel
Ranger Sta.

Administration Headquarters

Bright Angel Pt.

North Rim Lodge

BRIGHT ANGEL POINT
Post Office-Grand Canyon Lodge
Store-Camp Grounds-Garage

Travel across canyon by foot,
Muleback or Aeroplane only.

WALHALLA PLATEAU

CAPE ROYAL

AZTEC AMPHITHEATER

Pasture Wash
Ranger Sta.

Phantom Ranch

Cottages

Kaibab Suspension Bridge

KAIBAB NATIONAL FOREST

Hermits Rest

Bright Angel Lodge

El Tovar Hotel

Grand Canyon

Rowes Well
Tourist Camp

Observation Station
and Museum

Desert View Pt.

Checking Station

Public Camp Grounds
Desert View Watchtower

Wayside Museum
of Archaeology
and Tusayan Ruin

GRAND CANYON
SOUTH ENTRANCE

Post Office, El Tovar Hotel, Store, Bright Angel Lodge, Garage, Hospital, Hopi House, Cottages, Administration Building, General Information Office, Public Camp Grounds and Checking Station

Moqui Tourist Camp

Tusayan

Tourist Camp

Grandview Pt.

Buggeln Ranch

Hull Ranger
Sta.

COCONINO PLATEAU

KAIBAB NATIONAL FOREST

Anita Ranger Sta.

Anita

Red Butte
Airport

To Williams

10-L

Canyon Vista from Bright Angel Trail, Grand Canyon, Arizona. Bright Angel Canyon is as deep as the main canyon. Bright Angel Creek flows through Bright Angel Canyon and is a tributary of the Colorado River. Detroit Publishing Co., Phostint, circa 1920, $6-8.

Thor's Hammer, Grand Canyon, Arizona. Circa 1913, $5-7.

Little Colorado River Gorge, Grand Canyon.
Shown is a Fred Harvey Touring Car and some visitors.
Fred Harvey, Phostint, circa 1920, $6-8.

7521. Morning After a Storm, Grand Canyon, Arizona

Morning after a Storm, Grand Canyon, Arizona.
Fred Harvey, circa 1905, $6-9.

Grand Canyon, Arizona from Grand View Point.
Detroit Photographic Co., 1904, $7-9.

Up the Grand Canyon from Rowes Point. Newman Post Card Co., circa 1912, $6-8.

Climbing the Great Cliffs near head of Bright Angel Trail. Fred Harvey, Phostint, circa 1920, $6-8.

El Tovar Hotel

By 1901, train service began operating from Williams to the South Rim, and while Fred Harvey was not the first at the Grand Canyon to build a hotel or recognize the potential of tourism, he was the first to offer luxury accommodations at his hotel, the El Tovar. Guests paid three to five dollars per day on an American plan. He appointed his son Ford Harvey as El Tovar's manager to insure that the high standards of luxury plus value would ensure the success of the hotel. Hopi House, designed by Mary Jane Coulter, for Fred Harvey, was an unusual curio store. The architecture resembled an actual Hopi Pueblo and it became the place where visitors to the Grand Canyon could watch Native Peoples creating their arts and purchase their authentic items. The most popular items sold were baskets, Navajo rugs, silver and turquoise jewelry, pottery, and saddle blankets. Hopi artists lived in an apartment inside Hopi House and were required to perform a Hopi dance for visitors every afternoon, in addition to demonstrating their arts. Like the other employees of the early days, they often worked seven days a week.

El Tovar Hotel, Grand Canyon National Park.
El Tovar is located 7,000 feet above sea level and twenty feet from the South Rim of the Grand Canyon. Fred Harvey, circa 1925, $4-6.

Hotel El Tovar, Grand Canyon National Park.
El Tovar was designed by Charles Whittlesey to resemble a Swiss chalet combined with a hunting lodge. Because the hotel was constructed of Douglas fir logs, it was advertised as a large luxury cabin. The El Tovar opened in 1905 and was named for Spanish explorer Don El Tovar. Fred Harvey, circa 1920, $4-6.

The start from El Tovar on a Grand Canyon drive. Fred Harvey, 1906, $12-15.

Rendezvous Room Fireplace, Hotel El Tovar, Grand Canyon. Detroit Publishing Co., 1906, $8-10.

Verkamp's Souvenir Store, Grand Canyon National Park, Arizona is located east of the Hopi House. C. T. American Art Colored, circa 1930, $5-7.

Hotel El Tovar, Grand Canyon, Arizona.
The Rendezvous Room with Arts and Crafts style furniture, Navajo rugs, and animal heads mounted on the walls. Detroit Publishing Co., circa 1918, $6-8.

Ladies Lounging Room, Hotel El Tovar.
The purpose of the Ladies Lounging Room was to provide a place for ladies to chat, gossip, sew, read, and write letters. Fred Harvey, 1906, $10-14.

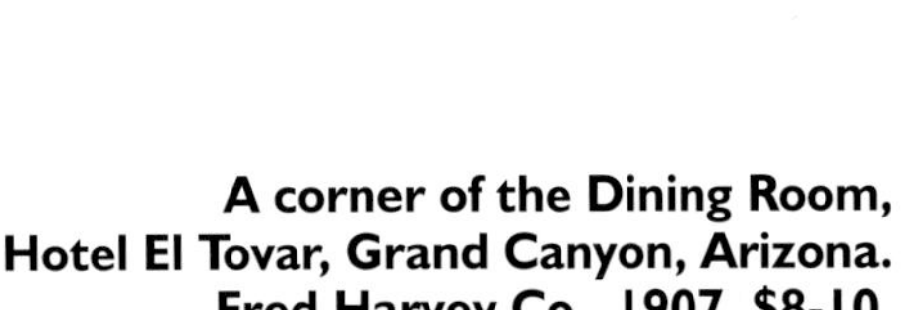
A corner of the Dining Room, Hotel El Tovar, Grand Canyon, Arizona. Fred Harvey Co., 1907, $8-10.

Hopi House, Grand Canyon, Arizona.
The Fred Harvey Hopi House was constructed of native stone and plastered with adobe. Fred Harvey, Phostint, circa 1920s, $4-6.

Main Room, Fred Harvey Hopi House, Grand Canyon, Arizona.
Fred Harvey, 1905, $8-10.

Fred Harvey Hopi House, Grand Canyon, Arizona.
Fred Harvey, 1906, $8-10.

Bright Angel Trail

The Bright Angel Trail begins on the South Rim and winds downward to Phantom Ranch and the Colorado River. The trail had been used by the Havasupai to obtain water and by prospectors who used burros to haul their supplies and ore. As the number of visitors who wanted access to the bottom of the canyon increased, mules were trained to carry visitors down the trail. Phantom Ranch Lodge was designed by Mary Jane Coulter for the Fred Harvey Company in 1922 to create permanent lodging for guests that came down to the river. Construction materials had to be packed down, and labor was done by hand. By the 1930s the Civilian Conservation Corps worked to improve the Bright Angel Trail, Phantom Ranch, and other trails in Grand Canyon.

Bright Angel Trail, Grand Canyon, Arizona. Detroit Publishing Co., Phostint, circa 1920s, $4-6.

The Devil's Corkscrew on Bright Angel Trail. Fred Harvey, circa 1930s, $4-6.

Indian Gardens, Bright Angel Trail. Fred Harvey, circa 1940s, $6-9.

Along the Cliffs on Hermit Trail. Fred Harvey, Phostint, circa 1930s, $5-7.

Indian Garden Camp, 3,180 feet below the Rim. This is the site of the original gardens farmed by the Havasupai. John G. Verkamp, circa 1915, $10-12.

Indian Gardens and Bright Angel Trail.
Fred Harvey, circa 1930s, $6-8.

Starting down the Grand View Trail, Grand Canyon, Arizona.
Detroit Photographic Co., 1902, $8-10.

On the Zigzags, Grand Canyon, Arizona. Detroit Photographic Co., 1902, $7-9.

The Fred Harvey Legacy

The Fred Harvey Company, with Mary Jane Coulter as chief architect, would continue to add new concessions to keep pace with the ever increasing number of tourists coming to the Grand Canyon.

Hopi Painting by Fred Kabotie, inside the Watchtower, Grand Canyon National Park, Arizona. Fred Harvey, 1940, $4-6.

The Kiva, at the base of the Watchtower, Desert View, Grand Canyon National Park, Arizona. Fred Harvey, circa 1944, $4-6.

The fireplace at Hermits' Rest, Grand Canyon National Park, Arizona. Set into a room forty-five feet wide and eighteen feet high, the rustic fireplace has a half dome shape. Fred Harvey, circa 1920s, $4-6.

The Watchtower at Desert View, located on East Rim Drive. C. T. Art Colortone, circa 1940s, $4-6.

The West Porch of Hermits' Rest, Grand Canyon. Hermit's Rest was designed by Mary Jane Coulter in 1914, and it is often considered the most creative building she designed. The site was tucked into a bluff, cut out of solid rock. Fred Harvey, circa 1920, $7-9.

Main Lodge of the Auto Cabin Camp, Grand Canyon National Park, Arizona. Fred Harvey, 1952, $5-7.

The Porch at Hermits' Rest, Grand Canyon National Park. Fred Harvey, Detroit Publishing Co., Phostint, circa 1930s, $5-7.

Hermit's Rest, Grand Canyon National Park. Hermit's Rest is perched on a cliff named for Louis D. Boucher, an old Canadian hermit, who built a camp on the South Rim using the native materials around him. Fred Harvey, circa 1940, $4-6.

The Lookout, Grand Canyon, Arizona.
Fred Harvey, Detroit Publishing Co., circa 1918, $5-7.

The Lookout Studio, Grand Canyon National Park, Arizona.
Fred Harvey, circa 1940s, $4-6.

Bright Angel Lodge on the Canyon's South Rim, Grand Canyon National Park, Arizona. Fred Harvey, circa 1940s, $4-6.

The Bright Angel Lodge

In the early days, John Hume had built a small lodge and cabins at the head of Bright Angel Trail. When Fred Harvey enjoyed an instant success with the El Tovar Hotel, plans were made in 1916 for a less expensive hotel to be named The Bright Angel. Because of the Great Depression, the plans were put on hold until 1934, when Mary Jane Coulter began the project. One notable feature that was in keeping with Coulter's ideas was that the buildings should draw from historical architecture. She hired people to find antique and rustic furnishings that had been brought to and used by early settlers in Arizona.

Coffee Shop, Bright Angel Lodge, Grand Canyon National Park, Arizona. Fred Harvey, circa 1940s, $6-8.

A Corner in the Lounge, Bright Angel Lodge, Grand Canyon National Park, Arizona.
The geological fireplace is ten feet high, and is made of native stones that are representative of the strata from the Colorado River bed to the South Rim. Fred Harvey, circa 1940s, $5-7.

H-4491—NATIVE DEER ON STEPS OF BRIGHT ANGEL LODGE, GRAND CANYON NATIONAL PARK, ARIZONA

Native deer can be seen on the steps of Bright Angel Lodge, Grand Canyon, Arizona. Fred Harvey, circa 1940s, $4-6.

The North Rim

Since the Grand Canyon National Park covers a vast area, there is a large variety of plant and animal species. The North Rim is almost a thousand feet higher in elevation than the South Rim, and the North Rim adjoins the Kaibab National Forest. Because of weather and road conditions, the season on the North Rim was late May to October.

Little Wild Horses, Grand Canyon, Arizona. RPPC, 1940, $6-8.

See this at Grand Canyon, Arizona.
A 2.5 by 3.5 inch advertising card distributed by the Kolb Brothers, "Shooting the Rapids" on the Colorado River. Kolb Brothers, 1937, $5-7.

GRAND CANYON NATIONAL PARK FROM THE TERRACE OF GRAND CANYON LODGE, ON THE NORTH RIM

**Grand Canyon National Park from the Terrace of Grand Canyon Lodge on the North Rim.
Union Pacific Railroad Pictorial Post Card, circa 1940s, $6-8.**

NEW UNION PACIFIC GRAND CANYON LODGE
NORTH RIM. GRAND CANYON NATIONAL PARK

**New Union Pacific Grand Canyon Lodge, North Rim.
Union Pacific Colorphoto, circa 1950, $10-12.**

Dining Room, Grand Canyon Lodge, North Rim. Union Pacific Colorphoto, circa 1951, $12-14.

Whitetail Kaibab Squirrel, Kaibab National Forest, Arizona. Union Pacific Railroad Pictorial Post Card, circa 1940s, $5-7.

Buffalo in Northern Arizona. A herd of nearly two hundred buffaloes grazing in House Rock Valley between the North and South Rims of the Grand Canyon. C. T. Art Colortone, circa 1940s, $5-7.

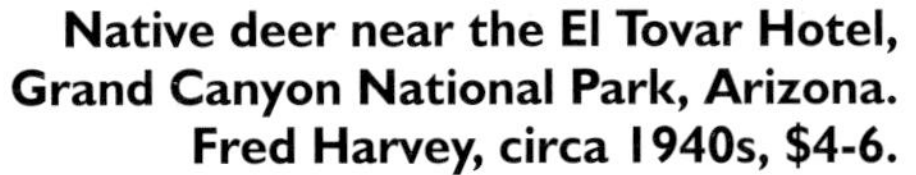

Native deer near the El Tovar Hotel, Grand Canyon National Park, Arizona. Fred Harvey, circa 1940s, $4-6.

Jacob Lake Post Office, Kaibab National Forest, Arizona. Frasher's Fotos, 1936, $8-10.

Scene in Kaibab National Forest, Arizona. Union Pacific Real Photo, circa 1940, $6-8.

**Jacob Lake Inn, Arizona.
A family business begun in the 1920s selling root beer to tourists grew to include an inn, cabins, and a restaurant. RPPC, 1937, $7-9.**

Kaibab Suspension Bridge over the Colorado River. Built in 1902, the suspension bridge was the only bridge for 1,000 miles north of Needles, California. The bridge was blown down during an unusual windstorm.
Fred Harvey, Detroit Publishing Co., Phostint, 1928, $6-8.

Wings over Grand Canyon. Photographic Section, Luke Field, Arizona.
C. T. Art Colortone, circa 1940s, $5-7.

Grand Canyon from the Air.
C. T. Art Colortone,
circa 1940s, $4-6.

Grand Canyon National Park:
The Watchtower at Desert View in Spring

Fred Harvey

Arizona's All-Year Vacation Land

GRAND CANYON NATIONAL PARK

Grand Canyon National Park is no seasonal playground. The South Rim of the Canyon is open all year—and, if you have never experienced it, a visit in fall, winter or spring will be a revelation to you. Summer crowds are gone, accommodations and sightseeing trips are readily available, and you can sit and watch the glorious Canyon colors (often more intense than in summer) at your leisure. The famous Rim Drives—East to The Watchtower, West to Hermit's Rest—are offered all year, and so are the spectacular Trail Trips by mule into the Canyon, which no visitor, having the opportunity, should miss. Ask the Transportation Desk for details.

GRAND CANYON SOUTH RIM OPEN ALL YEAR

May We Suggest A Glass or Bottle Of Wine With Your Order

Sauterne or Claret, glass .35 Carling's Red Cap Ale, Bottle .35

Eastern Beer, Bottle .35

WINE LIST ON REQUEST

A LA CARTE

Relishes

Prune Juice .25 Chilled Fruit Juice .25

Tomato Juice .25 Pickled Beets .20

Soup

Garden Fresh Vegetable Soup .25 Chicken Broth Egg Drops .25

ENTREES

Fluffy Omelette, Denver Style 1.00
Boston Baked Beans with Grilled Frankfurters 1.25
French Fried Fish Sticks, Tartar Sauce 1.15
Boiled Fresh Brisket of Beef, Horseradish Sauce 1.25
Pan Fried Round Steak, Country Gravy 1.35
Roast Arizona Turkey, Savory Dressing 1.50

A LA CARTE

Vegetables & Potatoes

Whipped Potatoes .25 Oven Brown Potato .25
French Fried Egg Plant .25 Creamed Celery .25

• SALAD •

Pulled Lettuce, Cheese Dressing .35

Sandwiches

Corned Beef Sandwich .65 Swiss on Rye .85 Ham or Tongue .75
American or Cheddar Cheese Sandwich .65
Deviled Ham Sandwich .65

• Desserts & Cheese •

French Apple Cobbler .25
Apple Pie .25 Layer Cake .20
Ice Cream .25, with Chocolate .35
Cheddar Blue Swiss or Camembert Cheese .50

• Beverages •

Milk .15 Coffee, Pot .25 Cup .15 Tea, Pot .25

Gin - Orange Juice
Cointreau

MULE TRAIN COCKTAIL 75¢

El Tovar Hotel

TABLE D'HOTE LUNCHEON

Monday, June 10, 1957

Choice of One

Prune Juice Tomato Juice Pickled Beets

Garden Fresh Vegetable Soup Chicken Broth Egg Drops

PRICE OF ENTREE DETERMINES COST

Fluffy Omelette, Denver Style 1.50
Boston Baked Beans with Grilled Frankfurters 1.75
French Fried Fish Sticks, Tartar Sauce 1.65
Boiled Fresh Brisket of Beef, Horseradish Sauce 1.75
Pan Fried Round Steak, Country Gravy 1.85
Roast Arizona Turkey, Savory Dressing 2.00

Whipped Potatoes Oven Brown Potato
French Fried Egg Plant Creamed Celery

SALAD

Pulled Lettuce, Cheese Dressing

Choice of One

French Apple Cobbler
Apple Pie Ice Cream Layer Cake
American Cheese Swiss Cheese

Coffee Tea Milk

Breakfast 7 to 9 Luncheon-12 to 2 Dinner 6 to 8

Arrangements gladly made for special diet. Suggestions or criticism regarding our service will be appreciated. We regret we cannot be responsible for the loss of wearing apparel or personal effects.

In addition to prices listed, 1% State Sales Tax will be collected.

May We Suggest A Glass or Bottle of Wine With Your Order
Sauterne or Claret, glass 35 Carling's Red Cap Ale, bottle 35
Eastern Beer, bottle 30

A LA CARTE

Appetizers

Orange Juice 25 Prune Juice 20 Ripe Olives 25 Hearts of Celery 25
Tomato Juice 20 Vegetable Juice 20

Salads

Fresh Shrimp with Lettuce 1.00 Lettuce and Tomato 45
Lettuce 35 Coleslaw 25

Potatoes & Vegetables

Dinner Potatoes 15 Dinner Vegetables 20

Desserts

Ice Cream 20, Sundae 30 Gelatin Dessert 15 Pie 25
Layer Cake 20 Pudding 20

- MELON IN SEASON 25 -

Beverages

Coffee, cup 10 Sanka 15 Postum 15 Milk 15 Tea, pot 15
Cocoa 20 Ovaltine 15

Sandwiches

Hamburger on Bun, Garnished 60
Cheeseburger on Bun, Garnished 65
Combination Chicken, Cheese on Rye, Dill Pickle, Coleslaw 1.00
Deviled Egg 40 Fried Egg 40 Chicken 90 Lettuce and Tomato 45

Fruit

Whole Orange 15 Sliced Orange 15 Stewed Prunes 20
Apple Sauce 20

In addition to prices listed 1% will be collected for state sales tax
Not responsible for loss of wearing apparel or personal effects

All prices are our OPS ceiling prices or lower.
A list showing our ceiling prices for each item is available for inspection.

Bright Angel Lodge
GRAND CANYON NATIONAL PARK, ARIZONA

Monday, July 21, 1952

LUNCHEON

Fruit Cocktail 40 Fresh Orange Juice 25
Shrimp Cocktail 75

Soup

Garden Vegetable Soup Chicken Broth with Rice
(Soup per cup 15 Bowl 25)

ENTREES

Cup of Soup or Tossed Lettuce with Egg Dressing
Poached Fillet of Rock Cod, Caper Sauce 1.00
Scrambled Ranch Eggs with Green Peppers .90
Poultry Livers and Fresh Mushrooms on Spaghetti, Caruso 1.15
Boiled Brisket of Corned Beef with New Cabbage 1.25
Crisp Potato Pan Cake, Rashor of Bacon, Apple Sauce 1.15
Assorted Delicatessen Plate (Bologna, Liverwurst, Salami, Swiss Cheese and Potato Salad) 1.25

(Rolls and Butter Served with Above Entrees)

(Choice of 1 Potato and 1 Vegetable)

Whipped Potatoes or Bouillon Potatoes
Lima Beans, Creole or Spiced Spring Beets

Desserts

Layer Cake 20 Pudding 20
Apple Pie 25 Gelatin Dessert 15 Ice Cream 20, Sundae 30

Beverages

Coffee, cup 10 Sanka 15 Postum 15 Milk 15 Buttermilk 10
Tea, pot 15 Cocoa 20 Ovaltine 15

View from "*Duck on the Rock*," Grand Canyon National Park, Arizona. Fred Harvey.

View from "Duck-on-the-Rock", Grand Canyon National Park, Arizona

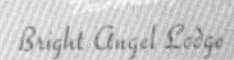

The Watchtower at Desert View is the climax of the famous Grand Canyon Rim Drive, which should not be missed by any visitor. Of all the incredible vistas studding the 32-mile scenic highway, Desert View is considered the finest. Located at the terminus of the East Rim Drive on the highest point of the South Rim, the Watchtower commands a spectacular view of the Canyon, the Colorado River, and of deserts, forests and mountains—a "magic circle" equaled by no other sight on earth.

GRAND CANYON NATIONAL PARK

in Arizona encompasses one of the world's greatest natural wonders—the titanic canyon for which it is named.

Cut by the turbulent Colorado River during millions of years, the Grand Canyon of today is 217 miles long, 4 to 18 miles wide, and a mile deep. Rising from its depths are whole ranges of mountains, ridges and intermediate plateaus slashed by hundreds of side canyons only slightly less incredible than the main gorge. Over the rock temples and majestic walls spreads a sea of ever-changing colors, ranging from the blue and purple shades of early morning and late evening to the brilliant yellow and vermilion hues of the noonday glare.

The South Rim of the Grand Canyon is easily reached by the Santa Fe Railway, or by automobile over Arizona Highway 64 branching off U. S. Highways 66 and 89.

Of the many activities and sightseeing trips offered to Grand Canyon visitors, the Grand Canyon Rim Drives provide the best opportunity to see much of the Canyon in a short time. An even more thrilling inspiration is an inner-canyon trip on muleback, an adventure no able-bodied visitor should miss.

All hotels and facilities on the South Rim are open throughout the year, and motor and trail trips are operated on a year-'round schedule.

GENUINE INDIAN CURIOS

Jacob Lake Inn carries a large stock of genuine Indian hand-made Rugs, Jewelry, Baskets and Pottery. Prices are reasonable and their real value lies in their absolutely genuine Indian manufacture, and in their beautiful natural coloring and original patterns.

Much of the Hopi and Navajo art is based on their superstitions and many of their designs bear a related significance, as in the "Storm" rug pattern, which carries out the symbols of geographical and tribal beliefs together with the "thunder bolt." While no two of these rugs are alike these symbols are woven into all rugs of this design.

Navajo rugs are made entirely by hand, every operation being done by the Indian women themselves, from the shearing of the sheep, the dyeing, carding, hand spinning (without the use of a wheel), and finally weaving on the hand-made looms. Both commercial and natural vegetable dyes are used.

Indian jewlery is made from coin or sheet silver, hand hammered and fashioned with crude instruments. A large number of beautiful designs are created, many of them including the use of turquois, the beautiful blue gem native of Arizona and New Mexico.

A great variety of baskets are made from grasses and willows, interweaving the natural colorings to produce beautiful and unusual designs.

All of the Indian pottery at Jacob Lake is absolutely genuine, being made by hand from clay, fired in primitive kilns and decorated with vegetable colorings applied with sticks. The "Thunder bird," sacred Hopi Indian bird is used extensively in pottery decoration.

Jacob Lake Inn, Kaibab Forest, Arizona

Chapter Three:

Highways and Byways

Transcontinental Highway between Boulder Dam and Kingman, Arizona.

Ashfork

Ashfork is located west of Williams and was named for the many ash trees that grew close to the town site. When the railroad junction was established, a settlement grew around it in 1883. The south branch of the railroad line carried ore from the mines around Prescott, and the railroad served the ranches around Ashfork by hauling cattle and supplies. Fred Harvey, in partnership with the Santa Fe Railroad, built the Escalante Hotel in 1905. While quite tiny by today's standards, the Escalante had twenty-six rooms, which made the Escalante one of Arizona's larger hotels in 1905.

The Escalante Hotel, Ash Fork, Arizona.
The Excalante was built in the style of California Missions. Fred Harvey, Detroit Publishing Co., Phostint, 1913, $5-7.

The Front of Hotel Escalante, Ash Fork, Arizona.
Fred Harvey, Detroit Publishing Co.,
Phostint, 1913, $5-7.

Cameron Trading Post

For the Native Peoples of Arizona, the trading post was not only a source of precious supplies, but also a place to sell or trade goods and a communal gathering place. A trading post would stock flour, sugar, canned goods, coffee, lard, cooking utensils, yard goods, Levi's, shoes, horse equipment, and other practical items. A system of pawn or holding jewelry, or other valuable items that could be redeemed with clipped sheep wool, animal hides, rugs, pinon nuts, or for sale jewelry was central to the trading post. A customer would receive a pawn ticket and was able to purchase goods until the pawn items could be redeemed or until said time of six to twelve months. The United States Government stopped the practice of pawn on the reservation in 1973, but it still continues by traders off the reservation. It was the trader's job to create a market for the artistic items he had bargained for. If a trader were a fair and honest person, he would often act as an advisor for business dealings between the Native Peoples and the United States Government.

Brothers Hubert and Dick Richardson built the Cameron Trading Post, located fifty-four miles north of Flagstaff on US Route 89, in 1916, after a one track suspension bridge was built over the Little Colorado River Gorge in 1911. Cameron is typical of the early trading posts that were built near a water source. Because Ralph Henry Cameron, Arizona's first senator, had been instrumental in getting the suspension bridge built, the trading post was named in his honor. The Fred Harvey Company opened the first road between the Grand Canyon and the Cameron Trading Post in 1923, because it was one of the few stopping places where guests could stay overnight. A hotel was constructed of native stone and had six guest rooms. Mabel Richardson designed terraced gardens behind the hotel, which was a real novelty in the area. Later a restaurant, service station, and motel were added. The original hotel is now a gallery for historical items from the local area, and Cameron continues to function much as it did in the early days by selling groceries and other practical items as well as promoting local arts and crafts.

Little Colorado Trading Post and Hotel, Cameron, Arizona — located fifty-five miles north of Flagstaff and forty miles from the Grand Canyon. Babbit Brothers Trading Co., 1931, $6-8.

Little Colorado Trading Post, Cameron, Arizona. Frasher's Fotos, 1937, $12-15.

Cameron Trading Post, Cameron, Arizona. Standard Oil Service Station, circa 1950, $25-30.

Cameron Hotel, Arizona. RPPC, L. L. Cook Co., circa 1948, $12-15.

Cameron Hotel, Arizona.
RPPC, L. L. Cook Co., circa 1948, $12-15.

Flagstaff

Flagstaff is located just a few miles from the San Francisco Peaks. The mountain range was named in 1629 by Franciscan missionaries in honor of St. Francis of Assisi. The San Francisco Peaks are the highest mountain range in Arizona. Mount Humphreys, the highest peak, is 12,633 feet, and was named for topographical engineer Brigadier General Andrew Atkinson Humphreys. The mountain range is a spiritual place for the Hopi and Navajo people, as it is believed to be the home of their spiritual gods. The mountain area is home to White and Silver fir, Yellow pine, Ponderosa pine, and Aspen. The area hosts a variety of wildlife such as White Tailed Deer, Rocky Mountain Mule Deer, Northern Elk, Coyotes, Black and Brown Bears, and Wild Turkeys.

When gold was discovered in California, Lt. Edward F. Beale and his men were given the task of finding a suitable wagon route that could be traveled year-round from New Mexico to California. One oddity of his successful expedition was the use of camels as pack animals. Beale surveyed old trails along the 35th Parallel and, by 1859 the Beale Wagon Road was in use. When it became known that the land in the area was suitable for logging and ranching, settlers began arriving. Settler Edward Whipple operated a saloon near the area that would become Flagstaff in 1871. A company of men hoping to farm the area arrived from Boston, and on July 4, 1876, they stripped a pine tree and hung the American flag to celebrate. Although circumstances forced the company of men to move on and they took their flag with them, the "flag staff" became a landmark, and the town that grew around it became known as Flagstaff. The wagon road that Lt. Edward Beale had surveyed was instrumental in the placement of the National Old Trails Highway in 1914.

National Old Trails Highway through Flagstaff, Arizona. Albertype, circa 1925, $8-10.

Greetings from Flagstaff, Arizona. C. T. Art Colortone, circa 1940s, $5-7.

Santa Fe Railroad Station, Flagstaff, Arizona. Albertype Co., 1923, $8-10.

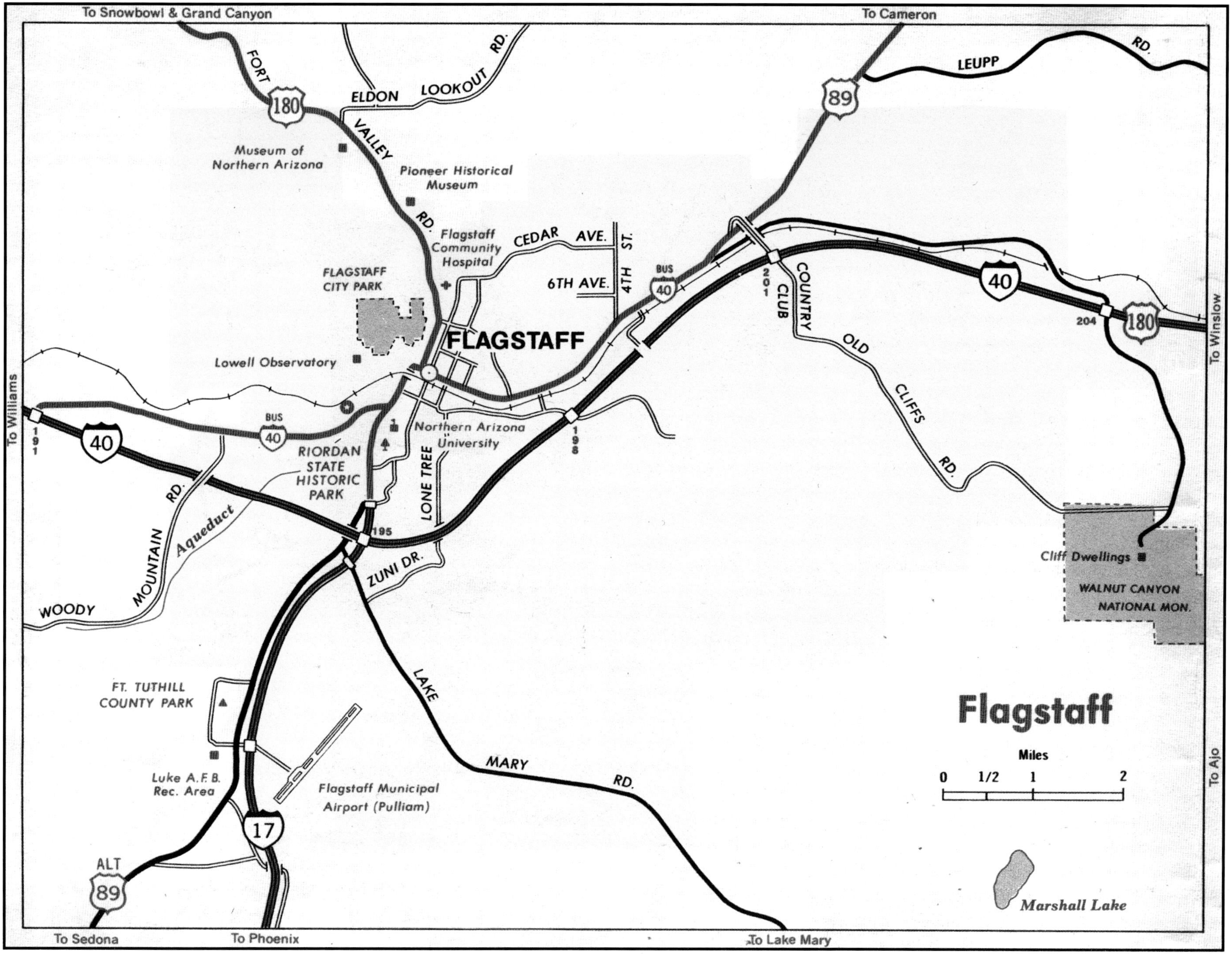

Flagstaff

To Snowbowl & Grand Canyon
To Cameron
To Williams
To Winslow
To Ajo
To Sedona
To Phoenix
To Lake Mary

FORT 180 VALLEY RD.
ELDON LOOKOUT RD.
LEUPP RD.
89
Museum of Northern Arizona
Pioneer Historical Museum
Flagstaff Community Hospital
CEDAR AVE.
4TH ST.
6TH AVE.
BUS 40
FLAGSTAFF CITY PARK
FLAGSTAFF
Lowell Observatory
201
COUNTRY CLUB
40
204
180
OLD CLIFFS RD.
191
40
BUS 40
Northern Arizona University
RIORDAN STATE HISTORIC PARK
LONE TREE
198
WOODY MOUNTAIN RD.
Aqueduct
195
ZUNI DR.
Cliff Dwellings
WALNUT CANYON NATIONAL MON.
LAKE MARY RD.
FT. TUTHILL COUNTY PARK
Luke A.F.B. Rec. Area
Flagstaff Municipal Airport (Pulliam)
17
ALT 89
Marshall Lake

Miles
0 1/2 1 2

San Francisco Peaks in the Coconino National Forest near Flagstaff, Arizona. C. T. Art Colortone, circa 1940s, $4-6.

Catholic Church and Parsonage, Flagstaff, Arizona. C. T. American Art, circa 1930s, $5-7.

San Francisco Peaks, Arizona. C. T. American Art Colored, circa 1930s, $4-6.

Lowell Observatory

The Lowell Observatory, founded in 1894, is one of the oldest observatories in the Southwest. The observatory is located on Mars Hill near downtown Flagstaff, and came into prominence in 1930 when astronomers at Lowell discovered the planet Pluto. By using the six telescopes at Lowell, the astronomers performed a number of studies on the canals on Mars, which were studied years later by the astronomers who worked on the Mariner space probes. Northern Arizona Teacher's College, which opened in 1899, became Northern Arizona University in 1966. The former National Old Trails Highway became a guideline for Route 66. Although Route 66 was just a gravel road in Arizona in 1926, it was a huge factor in the growth of the towns in Northern Arizona. The Mother Road, as Route 66 was nicknamed, spawned a whole new roadside industry of auto courts, cafes, curio stores, hotels, service stations, and roadside tourist attractions. Route 66 ran east and west through the heart of Flagstaff.

Northern Arizona Teachers College, Flagstaff, Arizona. C. T. American Art, 1930, $6-8.

Hotel Monte Vista, Flagstaff, Arizona—in the center of Northern Arizona's Playground. Associate Service Portraitone, circa 1949, $5-7.

Route 66, Flagstaff, Arizona. H. S. Crocker Co., circa 1953, $5-7.

Hotel Monte Vista, Flagstaff, Arizona. Western novelist, Zane Grey, who spent a lot of time writing in Northern Arizona, was one of the investors in this community-funded hotel. The Monte Vista was completed in 1927. C. T. American Art Colored, circa 1930s, $8-10.

Looking east on Santa Fe Avenue from Route 66, Flagstaff, Arizona. Petley, circa 1955, $5-7.

El Rancho Flagstaff Motor Hotel on Route 66. Colorpicture Publication, circa 1953, $6-8.

El Motel, US Highways 66 and 89, Flagstaff, Arizona. Tichnor Gloss, circa 1950, $6-8.

El Pueblo Motor Inn on US Routes 66 and 89, three miles east of Flagstaff. Dexter Press Silvercraft, circa 1950, $6-8.

Nackard Inn, Flagstaff, Arizona, one block south of US Route 66. Colorpicture Publication, circa 1940s, $6-8.

Dining Room of Gray Mountain Lodge, Flagstaff, Arizona. RPPC, circa 1952, $15-18.

Lava Beds and Sunset Mountain, US Route 66, Northern Arizona. C. T. Art Colortone, circa 1940s, $4-6.

Sunset Crater

Sunset Crater, located about twenty-nine miles northeast of Flagstaff, is evidence that a volcanic eruption occurred somewhere around 1064 AD. Scientists estimate that the volcanic eruption spewed nearly a billion tons of mater and ash into the air, building a cone about nine hundred feet high. While the base of Sunset Crater is formed of black lava and cinder, the cone area is composed of red and yellow particles from the final explosion of lava that contained large amounts of iron and sulphur. When John Wesley Powell was exploring Northern Arizona, he observed the crater at sunset when the sun's rays were highlighting the cone of the crater and it appeared to glow. He named it Sunset Crater.

Lava Beds and Sunset Crater, near Flagstaff, Arizona. Circa 1915, $8-10.

Sunset Mountain, extinct Volcano, near Flagstaff, Arizona. Fred Harvey, Detroit Publishing Co., Phostint, circa 1920s, $5-7.

Holbrook

Holbrook is located on the banks of Little Colorado River. In 1881-83 railroad tracks were laid and a train station was constructed. The town was named for H. R. Holbrook, who was the first chief engineer of the Atlantic and Pacific Railroad. When tick fever caused Texas cattle to be under a quarantine in 1885, cattle trains in great numbers began arriving in Holbrook, Winslow, and Flagstaff; as a result, Holbrook prospered as a cattle and railroad center that supplied the ranchers and trading posts. A famous shootout with cattle rustlers occurred at the Blevins House. Colorful saloons, such as the Bucket of Blood Saloon, were made famous by the many cowboys who drank there and the shootings that followed. By 1895, Holbrook became the county seat of Navajo County, and the Navajo County Courthouse and jail was built in 1898 in the Richardsonian Romanesque style at a cost of $15,000. Only one hanging in 1900, of murderer George Smiley, was known to have taken place there. In time, the cattle industry diminished, and America became a nation of automobiles, with US Route 66 running through the center of Holbrook. Since Holbrook is situated twenty miles from the Painted Desert and the Petrified Forest, many tourists stayed in Holbrook for more than one night. For tourists interested in "Indian Country," the Apache, Hopi, and Navajo Reservations are all a short drive.

Horned Toads, a day-old litter, Holbrook, Arizona. Holbrook Drug Co., 1938, $6-8.

Greetings from Holbrook, Arizona. J. R. Willis, 1946, $6-8.

Forest Motel, west side of US Highway 66, Holbrook, Arizona. Circa 1952, $6-8.

Commercial Hotel, Holbrook, Arizona. Rates are $1.25 and up; eighty-two clean comfortable rooms, each with hot and cold running water. D. T. Mallonee, circa 1930s, $15-18.

Court House, Holbrook, Arizona. Albertype Co., circa 1915, $10-12.

Kingman

The earliest residents in the area, which would become the city of Kingman, were the Hualapais and Mojaves. Kingman was named for Lewis Kingman, a railroad engineer for the Atlantic & Pacific Railroad. The railroad was extended to Flagstaff in 1882. While many of the towns around Kingman were created to support the gold and silver mines and were closed when the ore was depleted, Kingman continued to grow because of the railroad. By 1883, the town sites were designated and the twenty-four large city block town sites had a tax evaluation of $6,970. According to a newspaper article, Kingman was civilized by 1907 because the Board of Supervisors had passed a law to limit the houses of "ill repute" to operate more than one half mile from the Kingman schoolhouse, and all cattle, horses, and burros were prohibited from roaming the streets of Kingman.

View of Kingman from US Route 66, Arizona's Gateway to Boulder Dam. Albertype Co., circa 1936, $10-12.

Blanket Department, Hotel Beale, Kingman, Arizona. Albertype Co., circa 1930s, $20-25.

Kingman, Arizona, looking north on Fourth Street. Frasher's Fotos, circa 1948, $10-12.

Kingman, Arizona. Kingman has modern stores, auto courts, and very good restaurants. Royal Pictures. Circa 1954, $8-10.

Kingman was already a commercial center and a Route 66 town when construction began on Hoover Dam. Tourists who stayed in Kingman could travel to the Grand Canyon, west to California or north to Hoover Dam and Las Vegas. Kingman Army Airfield was established in 1945 during World War II as a gunnery-training base. It is estimated that over 35,000 individuals in the Army Air Corps were trained there. Following World War II, the former base became a storage and salvage yard for over 7,000 airplanes.

Kingman Grammar School. Albertype Co., published for Kingman Drug Store, circa 1930s, $6-8.

St. Mary's Catholic Church was built of native stone in 1906. Albertype Co., published for Kingman Drug Store. Circa 1930s, $6-8.

Odd Fellows Hall, Kingman, Arizona —located on the National Old Trails Highway. Albertype, circa 1920s, $6-8.

A Kingman Arizona Residence.
Fred Harvey, circa 1910, $10-12.

Post Office, Kingman, Arizona. Frasher's Fotos, 1944, $8-10.

Mojave County Courthouse, Kingman, Arizona.
RPPC, circa 1951, $8-10.

Arcadia Lodge, Route 66, Kingman, Arizona.
Colorpicture, circa 1940s, $6-8.

White Rock Court, US Highway 66, Kingman, Arizona.
The arrow points to Sleeping Dutchman rock formation in background.
MWM Bursheen, 1948, $5-7.

Bell Motel, US Route 66, Kingman, Arizona.
Colorpicture, circa 1940s, $6-8.

Angel Motel, Kingman, Arizona.
MWM Bursheen, circa 1940s, $5-7.

Wal-A-Pai Court, Kingman, Arizona, on US Route 66.
Associated Services, circa 1940s, $8-10.

Diamond H Rancho Courts, Kingman, Arizona.
Colorpicture, circa 1940s, $6-8.

Kingman Arizona Airfield. RPPC, circa 1950, $7-9.

Transcontinental Highway between Boulder Dam and Kingman, Arizona. Driving along the new highway that connects Kingman with Boulder Dam. C. T. Art Colortone. Circa 1938, $4-6.

Sedona

Early Sinaguans and Yavapai lived and farmed in Oak Creek Canyon located on the southwestern rim of the Colorado Plateau. The white limestone cliffs, red rocks, and lush vegetation of sycamores, alders, sumac, box elders, walnuts, oak, and pines made Oak Creek Canyon both a beautiful and practical area to hunt, gather, and farm. Oak Creek provided a source of water year-round and the mild climate provided ideal conditions for farming. Settlers began establishing their claims to the land in the area when The Homestead Act of 1862 encouraged Anglo-Americans to begin the process of establishing claims and improving the land. The first settler to file a claim to the land in Oak Creek Canyon was John J. Thompson in 1876. Unfortunately for Thompson, he later discovered he had made a mistake in the description of his claim and he was forced to begin again on another tract of land.

In Oak Creek Canyon, Arizona—the highway drops 2,000 feet in five miles, negotiating several switchbacks during the descent. C. T. Art Colortone, circa 1940s, $4-6.

Oak Creek, Arizona. Hand-colored. Circa 1920, $8-10

In Oak Creek Canyon on Alternate US Highway 89 between Prescott and Flagstaff, Arizona. C. T. Art Colortone, 1946, $4-6.

Oak Creek Canyon, Arizona.
The canyon walls are violet blue and vermillion.
One of the most scenic drives in the West.
Max Kegley, 1944, $6-8.

Oak Creek Canyon
—the most bewitching spot in Northern Arizona.
C. T. Art Colortone, 1944, $5-7.

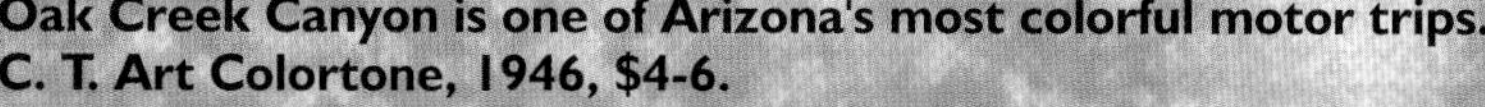

Oak Creek Canyon is one of Arizona's most colorful motor trips.
C. T. Art Colortone, 1946, $4-6.

Naming of the Town

The name Sedona came into being in 1902, when early settler T. Carl Schnebly applied to establish a post office in the area south of Oak Creek Canyon. The U.S. Postal Service rejected his two first choice names as too long. T. Carl's brother, Ellsworth Schnebly, suggested the name Sedona, who was T. Carl's wife. A road from Sedona through Oak Creek Canyon was completed in 1914 and the building of two bridges across Oak Creek in 1916 and 1917 made it easier for visitors to travel through Oak Creek Canyon. Sedona became home to farmers, cattle ranchers, hunters, and fishermen, but the filming of Zane Grey's novel, *The Call of the Canyon*, in 1923 would change the growth of Sedona forever. Westerns would continue to be filmed in Sedona for the next several decades, and by the time westerns were somewhat out of vogue, television crews were filming commercials.

Lower Oak Creek Canyon, Arizona —the location of America's most colorful motion pictures. C. T. Art Colortone, circa 1940s, $4-6.

Midgely Bridge, Oak Creek Canyon, Arizona. Petley, circa 1955, $4-6.

Harding's Pipe Organ,
Oak Creek Canyon, Arizona.
RPPC, circa 1951, $7-9.

Schnebly Hill, Oak Creek Canyon, Arizona. Circa 1950, $8-10.

Twin Peaks, Oak Creek Canyon, Arizona.
L. L. Cook Co., circa 1951, $6-8.

Sedona, Arizona.
This view shows the future site of Chapel of the Holy Cross.
Lollesgard Specialty Co., 1952, $4-6.

Cathedral Rock

The giant red rock formations were formed over a period of about 320 million years by eruptions, wind, and water. Cathedral Rock formation is the most photographed formation in Sedona. While most visitors view the east side of Cathedral Rock from Highway 179, the most spectacular view is from the west side, which overlooks Oak Creek. It was only natural that Sedona would attract artists in every medium. The landscape of red rocks, green juniper pines, an ever babbling creek, and interesting cacti under a clear blue sky is awe inspiring. Artists first began arriving in greater numbers in the early 1950s, and Sedona's art community has continued to flourish. Sedona artist, Margaurite Staude's memorial for her parents, the Chapel of the Holy Cross, attracts visitors from all over the world.

Castle Rock, Oak Creek Arizona.
While the photographer captioned the rock formation Castle Rock, this formation has been known for many years as Cathedral Rock.
RPPC, 1950, $5-7.

Cabins at Call of the Canyon Resort, Oak Creek Canyon, Arizona.
Frasher's Fotos, circa 1940s, $10-12.

Call of the Canyon Resort, in Oak Creek Canyon, was named for author Zane Grey's novel of the same name.
RPPC, Frasher's Fotos, circa 1940s, $10-12.

Chipmonk Store and Cabins, Upper Oak Creek Canyon, Arizona.
RPPC, circa 1950, $15-20.

Don Hoel's Cabins in the heart of Oak Creek Canyon, Arizona.
Circa 1953, $8-10.

Swimming Pool at Call of the Canyon Resort.
C. T. American Art, circa 1930s, $10-12.

Sedona, Arizona. Dexter Press, 1956, $4-6.

Sedona, Arizona.
H. S. Crocker Inc., 1955, $5-7.

Chapel of the Holy Cross, Sedona, Arizona. Petley, 1956, $5-7.

Chapel of the Holy Cross
—Built by Marguarite Brunswig Staude
as a memorial for her parents,
Margaurite and Lucien Brunswig.
Bob Plunkett, 1956, $6-8.

Greetings from Williams, Arizona—the Gateway to the Grand Canyon. C. T. Art Colortone, circa 1940s, $6-8.

Williams

Bill Williams Mountain, which reaches 9,282 feet, and the town of Williams were named for mountain man, fur trapper, and wandering preacher Old Bill Williams. Williams migrated to the west from North Carolina, riding on an Indian pony and wearing a buckskin suit and moccasins decorated with leather fringe. He was able to read and understand Apache signs. By the late 1800s, the area around Williams, Arizona had become a lumber, cattle ranching and railroad center. On September 17, 1901, the first steam train departed Williams station carrying supplies and passengers to the South Rim of the Grand Canyon. Soon Williams became known as The Gateway to the Grand Canyon. The Fred Harvey Company began construction on the Fray Marcos Hotel in 1908 using Francis W. Wilson as the architect; it was completed in 1910. The hotel had eight rooms available to the public and the rest were reserved for the Santa Fe Railroad employees. The train continued to operate until 1968, when most travelers chose to drive to the Grand Canyon. However, in 1989 the Grand Canyon Railway was brought back into service, and the former Fred Harvey Fray Marcos Hotel is now the depot for the Grand Canyon Railway. Williams was also a Route 66 town with its share of motels, cafes, and curio stores. Although a town in Texas was to have been the last Route 66 town to be bypassed by the Interstate, by a quirk of fate, Williams became the last official Route 66 town to be bypassed.

Bill Williams Mountain and Lake, Williams, Arizona. Detroit Publishing Co., Phostint, 1913, $4-6.

Bill Williams Mountain and Dam, Williams, Arizona. C. T. Art Colortone, 1954, $4-6.

Fray Marcos Santa Fe Hotel, Williams, Arizona. Fred Harvey, circa 1920, $6-8.

The Lobby, Fray Marcos Hotel, Williams, Arizona. Fred Harvey, circa 1915, $10-12.

Fray Marcos Santa Fe Hotel, Williams, Arizona. Detroit Publishing Co., Phostint, circa 1914, $6-8.

Fray Marcos Hotel, Indian Building, Williams, Arizona. Circa 1909, $10-12.

Air View of Bill Williams Mountain and Williams, Arizona. C. T. Art Colortone. Circa 1940s, $4-6.

Saginaw and Manistee Lumber Company's Mill, Williams, Arizona. C. T. Photochrome, circa 1920, $8-10.

Bird's Eye View of Williams, Arizona. Williams is the gateway to the Grand Canyon, the greatest of all the world's wonders. Fred Harvey, circa 1920s, $5-7.

Mt. Williams Court,
U.S. Highways 66 and 89,
Williams, Arizona.
Colorpicture ShiniColor,
circa 1952, $5-7.

Del Sue Motor Inn and Service Station,
on US Highway 66, Williams, Arizona.
MWM Bursheen, circa 1940s, $6-8.

Westerner Motel, Williams, Arizona.
Tichnor Brothers Tichnor Gloss, circa 1954, $5-7.

Winslow

The town of Winslow began when a railway station for the A & P Railroad was established in 1881. A debate exists whether the town was named for the Arizona prospector Tom Winslow or for Edward Winslow, the president of the Saint Louis/San Francisco Railroad. Winslow became an important shipping point for the Santa Fe Railroad. The Fred Harvey Company opened a Harvey House in Winslow, and like the other Harvey Houses, it was well known for fine dining, served by well-trained Harvey Girls along the Santa Fe Railroad. In addition to shipping the freshest ingredients by refrigerated rail cars for his menus, the Fred Harvey philosophy was to add extra value. The Fred Harvey House sandwiches always contained generous ingredients and a third slice of bread was placed in the middle to make each sandwich have extra value. Following the success of the other Fred Harvey Hotels, plans were made to open a hotel named La Posada in Winslow very close to replace the Fred Harvey House. Mary Jane Coulter designed La Posada, which means 'the resting place' in Spanish, at a cost of one million. The seventy-room, 60,000 square foot hotel was completed in 1929, when Winslow was the largest town in Northern Arizona. By 1957, the age of railroad travel had declined to the point that La Posada was closed. A portion of the hotel was still used by the Santa Fe Railroad as offices. La Posada was purchased in 1997 and restored. Today, a stay at La Posada is a must for those interested in historic hotels and railroad history. Winslow was also a Route 66 town and was the closest town for guests visiting Meteor Crater.

8,000 Nice People Welcome You to Winslow, Snake Dance Country, Arizona. Petley, 1953, $4-6.

Santa Fe Station and Harvey House Hotel, Winslow, Arizona. Fred Harvey, 1909, $8-10.

Fred Harvey
LA POSADA
WINSLOW, ARIZONA

A refreshing oasis on the way to and from Grand Canyon National Park
La Posada
WINSLOW ARIZONA
A Fred Harvey HOTEL
OPEN THE YEAR ROUND

La Posada Dining Room, Fred Harvey Hotel, Winslow, Arizona. Fred Harvey, circa 1940s, $4-6.

H-4158 DINING ROOM, LA POSADA, FRED HARVEY HOTEL, WINSLOW, ARIZONA

H-4224 LA POSADA, FRED HARVEY HOTEL, WINSLOW, ARIZONA

La Posada, Fred Harvey Hotel, Winslow, Arizona. La Posada was built in the low rambling style introduced into the Southwest by the early Spanish immigrants. Fred Harvey, circa 1940s, $4-6.

H-4159 THE LOUNGE, LA POSADA, FRED HARVEY HOTEL, WINSLOW, ARIZONA

La Posada Lounge, Fred Harvey Hotel, Winslow. The Lounge has high-backed chairs and hand-carved davenports. Some are authentic and some are replicas. Fred Harvey, circa 1940s, price unknown.

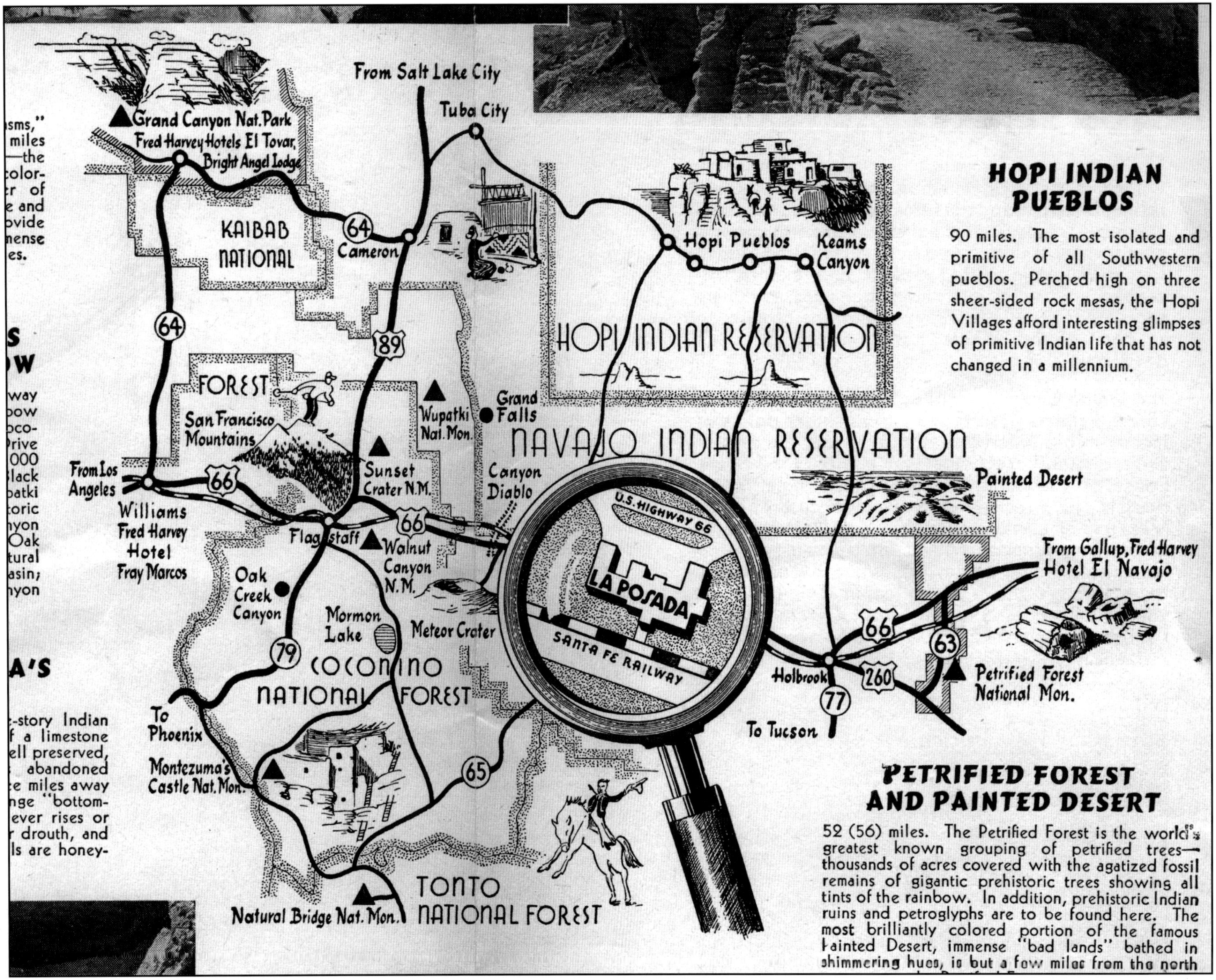

isms,"
miles
—the
color-
r of
e and
ovide
nense
es.

S
W

way
pow
oco-
Drive
000
Black
patki
toric
nyon
Oak
tural
asin;
nyon

A'S

-story Indian
f a limestone
ell preserved,
abandoned
e miles away
nge "bottom-
ever rises or
r drouth, and
ls are honey-

From Salt Lake City
Tuba City
Grand Canyon Nat. Park
Fred Harvey Hotels El Tovar, Bright Angel Lodge
KAIBAB NATIONAL
64
Cameron
89
FOREST
San Francisco Mountains
Wupatki Nat. Mon.
Grand Falls
Sunset Crater N.M.
From Los Angeles
66
Williams
Fred Harvey Hotel Fray Marcos
Flagstaff
Walnut Canyon N.M.
Canyon Diablo
Oak Creek Canyon
Mormon Lake
Meteor Crater
79
COCONINO NATIONAL FOREST
To Phoenix
Montezuma's Castle Nat. Mon.
65
TONTO NATIONAL FOREST
Natural Bridge Nat. Mon.
Hopi Pueblos
Keams Canyon
HOPI INDIAN RESERVATION
NAVAJO INDIAN RESERVATION
Painted Desert
U.S. HIGHWAY 66
LA POSADA
SANTA FE RAILWAY
From Gallup, Fred Harvey Hotel El Navajo
66
63
Holbrook
260
77
To Tucson
Petrified Forest National Mon.

HOPI INDIAN PUEBLOS

90 miles. The most isolated and primitive of all Southwestern pueblos. Perched high on three sheer-sided rock mesas, the Hopi Villages afford interesting glimpses of primitive Indian life that has not changed in a millennium.

PETRIFIED FOREST AND PAINTED DESERT

52 (56) miles. The Petrified Forest is the world's greatest known grouping of petrified trees—thousands of acres covered with the agatized fossil remains of gigantic prehistoric trees showing all tints of the rainbow. In addition, prehistoric Indian ruins and petroglyphs are to be found here. The most brilliantly colored portion of the famous Painted Desert, immense "bad lands" bathed in shimmering hues, is but a few miles from the north

Highway across Boulder Dam, connecting Nevada and Arizona.
C. T. Art Colortone, circa 1940s, $4-6.

Hoover Dam

Before Hoover Dam was begun in 1931, the Colorado River was an unpredictable force that supplied water to the seven states of Arizona, California, Colorado, Nevada, New Mexico, Utah, and Wyoming. An over abundant snowfall could create devastating flooding, while in summer the river would slow to a trickle. In 1922, an agreement, named *The Colorado River Compact,* was reached between the states that stated how the water would be equitably allotted. Plans were made for the construction of storage dams including Hoover Dam. The dam was to be constructed about thirty-five miles from Las Vegas. A super construction company formed of six companies, appropriately named Six Companies Inc., was hired by Congress and construction began in 1931 during the Great Depression. Even under the harsh and dangerous working conditions, people arrived from all over the United States hoping for any work available. Wages varied according to the type of work and the level of skill needed. In general, the wage scale ranged from fifty to eighty-two cents per hour. There were only two days of the year that work stopped and they were the 4th of July and Christmas. One hundred workers died during the construction of the dam, but it is only a myth that there are workers buried in the dam.

Boulder Dam
—upstream face and Intake Towers from the Arizona side.
C. T. Art Colortone, circa 1940s, $4-6.

Lowering loaded Box Car, Boulder Dam.
C. T. Art Colortone, circa 1940s, $4-6.

Opening of Twelve Valves, from below, Boulder Dam. Herz, circa 1940s, $4-6.

Arizona Spillway, Boulder Dam, Boulder Canyon.
This was a project of the Bureau of Reclamation.
C. T. Art Colortone, circa 1940s, $4-6.

Although the construction of Hoover Dam was expected to take over seven years, the dam was completed in five years at a cost of $49 million. Hoover Dam is 726 feet high, 1,244 feet long, and was constructed of 4.4 million cubic yards of concrete. Newswriters estimated that if that amount of concrete had been used to construct a two-lane road, the road would have stretched for 3,300 miles long. Hoover Dam has a storage capacity of 28.5 million-acre feet, which equals 9.2 trillion gallons of water. The operation of the dam is supported from the sale of the hydroelectric power generated by the power plant at the dam. At the dedication of the dam on September 30,1935, the name of the dam was Boulder Dam, since the name of the construction project had been the Boulder Canyon Project. However, in 1947, Congress voted to change the name to Hoover Dam, named for Herbert Hoover, the thirty-first President of the United States, because he had been a strong advocate for the construction of the dam. Today, Hoover Dam is a National Historic Landmark and was named the fifth most important construction project of the twentieth century. Over one million people visit Hoover Dam each year.

Figures of the Republic, Hoover (Boulder) Dam. C. T. Art Colortone, 1953, $6-8.

Sunset at Boulder Dam. C. T. Art Colortone, circa 1940s, $4-6.

Hoover Dam and Powerhouse, with Fortification Mountains in distance, Colorado River. C. T. Art Colortone, circa 1940s, $4-6.

Visitors' Gallery inside Hoover Dam. C. T. Art Colortone, circa 1940s, $5-7.

Bibliography

Barnes, Christine. *El Tovar at Grand Canyon National Park*. Bend, Oregon: W. W. West Inc., 2001.

Barnes, Will C. *Arizona Place Names*. Tucson, Arizona: University of Arizona Press, 1960.

Berke, Arnold. *Mary Coulter, Architect of the Southwest*. New York, New York: Princeton Architectural Press, 2002.

Brown, Robert H. *Sedona: Arizona's Red Rock Community*. Phoenix, Arizona: The Bronze Age Publishers, 1993.

Clark, Victoria. *How Arizona Sold Its Sunshine, Historical Hotels of Arizona*. Sedona, Arizona: Bluegourd Publishing, 2004.

Dedera, Don. *Navajo Rugs, How to Find, Evaluate, Buy, and Care for Them*. Flagstaff, Arizona: Northland Press, 1975.

Eddington, Patrick and Susan Makov. *Trading Post Guidebook*. Flagstaff, Arizona: Northland Publishing, 1995.

Hegemann, Elizabeth C. *Navaho Trading Days*. Albuquerque, New Mexico: University of New Mexico Press, 1963.

Malach, Roman. *Century of Kingman 1882-1982*. Kingman, Arizona: Mohave County Board of Supervisors, 1982.

Sides Smith, Dorothy. *Decorative Art of the Southwestern Indians*. New York, New York: Dover Publications Edition, 1961.

Trimble, Marshall. *Arizona, A Panoramic History of a Frontier State*. Garden City, New York: Doubleday & Company. Inc., 1977.

Witzel, Michael Karl. *Route 66 Remembered*. Osceola, Wisconsin: Motorbooks International, 1996.

Index